Cley Marsh and its Birds

CLEY MARSH AND ITS BIRDS

Second Edition

Billy and Bernard Bishop

HILL HOUSE PRESS

Published by Hill House Press Ltd
Coast Road, Cley, Holt, Norfolk NR25 7RZ

First Edition Published 1983
by The Boydell Press
ISBN 0 85115 180 9

Second Edition 1996

© Billy Bishop 1983
© Bernard Bishop 1996

ISBN 0 9528031 0 0

Cover illustration by Robert Gillmor

This book is copyright and may not be reproduced, stored or transmitted by any means without prior permission of the publisher.

A catalogue record for this book is available from the British Library

Printed and bound by Page Bros (Norwich) Ltd

CONTENTS

List of Illustrations   *vii*
Preface and Acknowledgements   *viii*
First Edition Acknowledgements   *ix*
Foreword to the first edition by HRH the Duke of Edinburgh   *xi*
Map of the Reserve   *xii*
Introduction   1
The Good Old Days?   8
The Old-Time Wildfowlers   15
Local Relations   29
Bringing Back the Lost Species   31
New and Rare Birds   39
Weather Lore   42
The Menace of Vermin   45
A Warden's Life   50
Some Tips on Identification   59
Extracts from the Warden's Diary 1937 - 1981   63
Extracts from the Warden's Diary 1982 - 1996   81
Checklist   96
Appendix: The History of Cley Marshes   141

ILLUSTRATIONS

1. C.D. Borrer and Frank Izod Richards
2. The old 'Britannia'
3. A case from the Richards collection
4. H.N. Pashley
5. E.C. Arnold
6. Ted Ramm
7. Dr Sidney Long
8. The sale by auction of Cley Marshes
9. The purchase by Dr Long
10. Robert Bishop
11. Billy Bishop with Bittern chick
12. With Major Aubrey Buxton
13. A seal cull with Ted Eales
14. With Lord and Lady Alanbrooke and Dick Bagnall-Oakeley
15. The 1953 Flood: Cley village
16. The 1953 Flood: The Reserve
17. A Coypu hunt
18. Billy and Bernard Bishop at work
19. The opening of the Dick Bagnall-Oakeley Memorial Centre
20. The 1996 Flood: The new hides
21. The 1996 Flood: At Old Woman's Lane
22. The clear-up: Bernard Bishop
23. NWT salvage team at the Coast Road
24. HRH The Prince of Wales with Bernard Bishop, March 1996

PREFACE
AND
ACKNOWLEDGEMENTS

This new edition includes the main text of my father's book as originally published in 1983. With the addition of new material, this second edition is intended to give a comprehensive and up-to-date view of the Reserve's history and birdlife.

I have added new diary entries for the years 1982 - 1996. The original Checklist notes have been reprinted, with additional comments and notes to reflect changes in status and more recent records. Notes on species new to the locality since 1983 have been added.

The recent history of the Reserve is described in the Introduction.

For their help in preparing this second revised edition, I would like to express special thanks to Lord Buxton, Joe Johnson, and Don and Mary Dorling.

FIRST EDITION
ACKNOWLEDGEMENTS

I would like to express my grateful thanks to all my many friends who have helped in the preparation of this book.

My thanks are due to Colin Willock, who edited and gave me professional advice on my manuscript, and to his secretary, Gillian Conway, who typed the final version. Especial thanks also to Michael Seago, for his help in ensuring the completeness of the list of Birds of Cley; Ken McKillop for his great patience in reading my notes; Miss Hilary Webb, for spending many hours typing them, helped by my daughter-in-law, Christine. Mrs Mary Catlin for allowing me access to the notes of her late husband, Peter, who, like me, was the son of a henchman to the 'Gentlemen Gunners'.

I am grateful to Miss Pat Luckett, Mrs Eileen Parrinder, and Mrs Judy McKillop for all the encouragement given to carry on when I had often felt like giving up.

Finally, my grateful thanks to the son and daughter of my great friend the late Dick Bagnall-Oakeley, namely Jane Ann and Jeremy, who made it possible to include some of their father's photographs.

I would also like to thank the lucky star under which I was undoubtedly born. I have been so fortunate in having been able to earn my livelihood in an adult occupation which was simply a continuance of my schoolboy hobby, an occupation which has given me a great sense of satisfaction.

I have a sense of fulfilment when, looking out of my house which The National Naturalists Trust built for me on my retirement, I gaze over the marsh that has been my responsibility to develop into one of the finest reserves in our country and which my son Bernard has now taken on.

This book is, in a sense, a tribute to my own good fortune and to all those innumerable friends, acquaintances and visitors whom it has been my lifelong pleasure to meet and welcome at Cley.

BUCKINGHAM PALACE.

Anyone who has had the pleasure of wildfowling or bird-watching on the Norfolk coast knows about the Cley Marshes and Billy Bishop, or perhaps I ought to put it the other way round because without him Cley would not be what it is today.

I daresay there are lots of people who believe they are creating the Britain of the future, planners, developers, social reformers and such like, but the fact that there is so much to enjoy in the country today is largely due to people like Billy Bishop. He is one of the few who have written about his life but thank goodness there are thousands, hundreds of thousands like him whose natural sympathy and care for their local countryside has done so much to blend the human occupation of the land with the natural environment. This empathy comes out in every line in this book.

I freely admit that I am prejudiced but I find it difficult to believe that anyone who values our countryside will not thoroughly enjoy Billy's memories.

1982

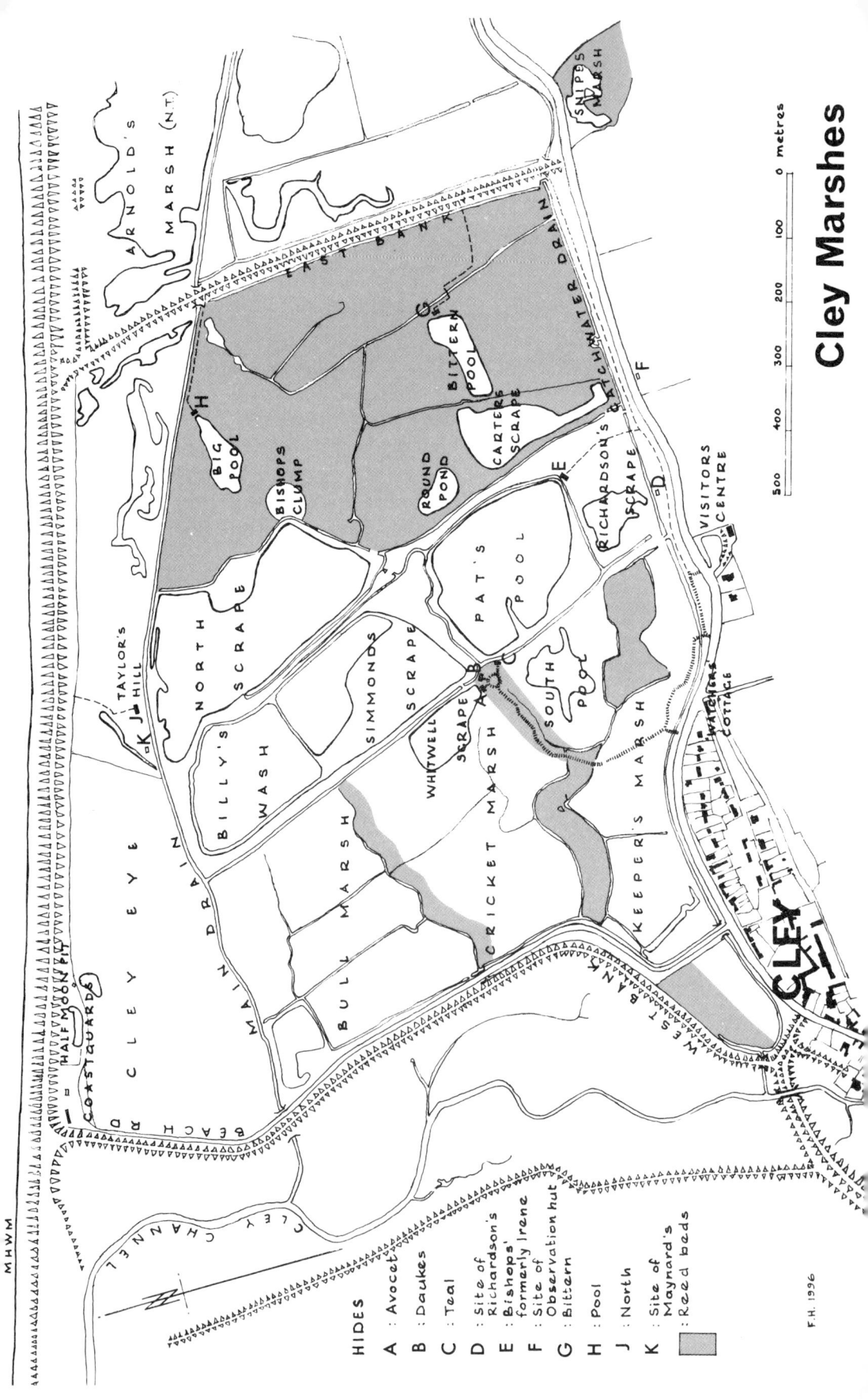

Cley Marshes

HIDES
A : Avocet
B : Daukes
C : Teal
D : Site of Richardson's
E : Bishops' formerly Irene
F : Site of Observation hut
G : Bittern
H : Pool
J : North
K : Site of Maynard's

Reed beds

F.H. 1996

Introduction

When my father published these memoirs in 1982 he had seen, in the course of a lifetime, Cley Marsh transformed. Indeed he himself had been responsible for much of the change.

Though it had been managed as a reserve since 1926, shooting continued on the marsh until the mid-sixties. The job of Warden (or Watcher as it was called in the early days) was as much about keeping pools open for shooting in the winter as it was about maintaining a habitat for breeding birds. Until the mid-sixties there were no observation hides and very few visitors.

The marsh, when I was a child, was a very private place and looking back (no doubt through rose-tinted spectacles) it was a wonderful environment to grow up in. As a boy I certainly spent as much time as possible with father, 'helping' with whatever job was under way. My memories are of joining in the reed-cutting in the winter and taking the cut reed off the marsh by boat along the dykes to be loaded onto lorries at the roadside; of the dykes being cleared by hand with drag-lines. On Sundays in the summer we would row my grandfather's boat out from Cley Quay to Blakeney Point when the tide was right - we called them 'Point Sundays'. We would chat with the Warden Ted Eales then anchor out in the Harbour to catch flat-fish on the first of the tide. At migration time I would help Richard Richardson with ringing at his Heligoland trap on the Walsey Hills. In the autumn there were pigeon shoots on Cley Hall farm, and the owner Major Blount never objected to boys bagging the odd rabbit for the pot provided we got up to no mischief.

Looking back on those days in the 1950's and early 1960's it does seem that the sun shone every day.

*

By this time attitudes to conservation were changing quite rapidly. In 1964 the Reserve was declared a Bird Sanctuary under the 1954 Act which brought an end to shooting on Cley Marsh.

The first observation hides were built in that year, and by 1966 my father was commenting in a newspaper article on what a busy year it had been - with no less than 600 visitors using the new hides! Over the next few years new scrapes were dug out and more hides were built. The number of visitors exploded, and dealing with the public increasingly became a major part of the Warden's life. There was, of course, still routine maintenance and reed-cutting to be done, and there were still all-night vigils on the marsh to combat egg-collectors. It soon became clear to the Trust that the services of an Assistant Warden were needed.

I count myself very fortunate to have been appointed to that post in 1972.

With manpower doubled, the pace of change quickened over the next few years: Carter's Scrape and North Scrape were both enlarged, Simmond's Scrape and Pat's Pool were dug out, and Maynard's and Irene Hides were built. By the time my father retired in 1979, the Reserve had very broadly taken on the shape and form we see today.

*

Nonetheless, there were some major developments to come in the 1980's and '90's. When I became Warden there were certainly many improvements I was keen to carry out when funds permitted. The first job I tackled was a relatively small one, but it brought considerable benefits.

Very little water was getting through to the reed-beds along the East Bank. The reed was getting clogged up and was deteriorating. So we dug a new drain from the car-park the whole length of the reed-bed bringing fresh water from the springs into that eastern edge of the reed. This not only had the effect of revitalising the reed and increasing insect life, it also provided some extra security. It had previously been

INTRODUCTION

possible to walk straight into the reed-bed from the East Bank without too much difficulty. Egg collectors were still a problem at this time and any work that made life more difficult for them was obviously worthwhile. But it also brought more privacy to that part of the Reserve, given the huge number of people (and their dogs) using the East Bank.

This sort of work is unspectacular, but is vitally important in maintaining the habitat with ever-increasing numbers of visitors to the Reserve.

1979 also saw the opening of the Public Hide by the Coast Road in memory of the naturalist and artist Richard Richardson. A new pool was dug out in front of it, and almost the first bird I saw on it was a Wilson's Phalarope - a beautiful bird which had only once before been recorded at Cley. Despite this auspicious beginning, the pool has not attracted birds to any great degree, perhaps largely due to the fact that we were unable to control the water-level.

Whitwell Scrape was the next area to be dug out and Avocet Hide was built overlooking it, in memory of Godfrey Whitwell who, with his wife Sylvia, had been a great supporter of the Trust. This completed the trio of hides and system of scrapes that form the main focus for visitors to the Reserve.

More large-scale work followed over the next few years. One of my father's greatest ambitions had been fulfilled with the successful breeding of Avocets in 1977. They had mostly been using North Scrape which was still quite small at the time of his retirement. Over the winter of 1982-83 we were able to do a really quite colossal amount of work extending the scrape southwards, more than doubling its size and, at the same time, lowering the small islands created from the original spoil to form more suitable breeding conditions for the Avocets.

The next large development came in 1987 with the creation of a wet area in memory of my father (see Diary entry). The section of grazing marsh, more or less in the centre of the Reserve, was dug out quite deep in order to get fresh water onto the area. The intention was to encourage breeding by Black-tailed Godwit. Father had long hoped to see these birds breeding at Cley. Over the years they had nested occasionally on various parts of the Reserve, but had never bred successfully. To date we have still had little success with Godwits, though they have shown great interest in the area and on many occasions we have thought they were preparing to nest. The problem may well be that they require more space. Cley Reserve is only about 400 acres and contains three distinct types of habitat. Reed-bed and open water form quite a high proportion, leaving a relatively small area of grazing marsh. Certainly their breeding grounds in Holland are enormous areas compared with Cley where, of course, they also have to contend with a degree of disturbance from people using the paths, the banks and the shingle ridge.

But the Cricket Marsh, between Whitwell Scrape and the Beach Road, is another area we've managed to get water onto, and they have also attempted to nest there. Unfortunately they have so far been thwarted by predators. So we live in hope of breeding by Black-tailed Godwit. There is certainly now an area of suitable habitat with the potential for success.

The Bittern is another bird that is very special to Cley, and was dear to my father's heart.

Since breeding for the first time at Cley in 1937 numbers have fluctuated between one and five booming males. They are hard hit by severe winters and by the effects of salt-water flooding, and some years they have not bred at all.

As a British breeding species it is, of course, exceptionally vulnerable, as is its natural habitat. In 1995 the RSPB identified only twenty booming males in the country, and a new partnership project was announced involving the Wildlife Trusts, the RSPB and English Nature in an attempt to encourage breeding.

Norfolk is obviously an important part of the project and work is being carried out all along the north Norfolk coast, at Titchwell, Holme and Blakeney, as well as on the Broads where water-levels are being raised to create larger areas of wet reed-bed.

At Cley, two factors mean that we have to take a different approach. Firstly, we have dry reed-beds which are always under threat of encroachment by bramble, scrub and grass. Secondly, in recent years we have experienced very dry summers, with relatively little rainfall in winter. Our solution is to dig out the base of reed-beds that are suffering from encroachment, effectively lowering the bed by a few inches. This allows us to flood these areas and keep the water-level

INTRODUCTION

under control, maintaining a deeper, wetter base in which reed can flourish.

The second, and equally important part of the project at Cley consists in 'reprofiling' both the edges of scrapes and pools, and the dyke system within the reed-bed. Our dykes and ditches have always been steep-sided, which effectively cuts them off as feeding areas. By reprofiling the sides to a gentle slope, reed will grow down to the water's edge providing both easy access and cover for the Bitterns to feed.

The cost of the work, particularly removal of the spoil, is enormous and the project is likely to take several years to complete. But work is under way in what we class as the most sensitive areas.

The Round Pond, which was originally a wildfowling pool, has always been a wet area. That has been redug so that it forms a secluded pool within the reeds. For some reason young Bitterns tend to favour the northern end of Carter's Scrape as a feeding area, so we have now reprofiled the edges, allowing it to become a reed-fringed pool.

Bittern Pool has been dug out, together with an area to the north of Bittern Hide, and new pipework has been put in so that we can flood it with fresh water.

Another high priority area favoured by Bitterns lies between North Scrape and the Pool Hide.

All in all the work the Trust hopes to carry out may take a decade to complete. Doing it gradually, phase by phase, does at least have the great merit of keeping disturbance of the marsh to a minimum.

So far as the birdlife of the Reserve is concerned, The Bittern Project is undoubtedly the most exciting development at Cley for many years, particularly since it should benefit other secretive species requiring a habitat of reed-bed and shallow water, such as Water Rail and Spotted Crake.

*

But from the point of view of the visitor, there was another very pressing need.

For some time we had been painfully aware that the hides and boardwalks were reaching a point where effective repair was no longer an option. Maintenance was becoming a nightmare. We were constantly replacing pieces of timber and board, jacking up sections of boardwalk and inserting lumps of wood in an effort merely to keep things going.

But the plain fact was that hides, some of which had been in place for thirty years, were now too small, built at a time when the Reserve received only a tiny fraction of the number of visitors that come nowadays. As for the boardwalks - some sections had deteriorated to the point where they were becoming potentially dangerous. Something had to be done.

The small committee charged with formulating a plan initially came up with an improvement scheme that was very ambitious. Apart from upgrading the hides and access to them, it included a very much enlarged Visitors' Centre housing a shop and information centre, accommodation for an Assistant Warden, a workshop and public toilets. Planning permission for a scheme on this scale was turned down, and our attention focused on the crucial elements of the plan - improving facilities for visitors within the Reserve itself.

The scaled-down scheme provided for new boardwalks that would allow wheelchair access, three new hides replacing the Daukes complex, together with replacements for Irene and North Hides. As part of the package the planners asked for the removal of some existing hides. These were Maynard's, the old Billy's Hide and Richardson's - none of which was really a great loss.

This scheme was accepted and, with the success of the Dr Sidney Long Appeal launched to raise funds to carry out the scheme, work began in the autumn of 1995 with the removal of Maynard's and Richardson's Hides.

Of the three central hides, Daukes and Avocet were dismantled and solid concrete bases were laid as a foundation for their replacements. I've always found suspended wooden floors quite unsatisfactory. Every movement within the hide causes vibration through the floor which is transmitted directly to tripods and telescopes. So I was determined from the start that our new hides would have good solid bases. As for roofing, the decision was taken to thatch them using reed we had cut ourselves at Cley together with sedge from another of the Trust's reserves on the broads.

By the New Year work had progressed well enough for thatching to commence on Daukes Hide. New boardwalks had been laid and by

INTRODUCTION

mid-February everything seemed on course for the official opening of the new facilities by Prince Charles on March 28th.

Gales and exceptional tides on February 19th and 20th were to play havoc with those plans. I have described the floods that ensued in the Diary section. Suffice it to say here that thanks to the extraordinary efforts of a large number of people, and an amazingly swift and generous response to the Disaster Appeal, the boardwalks were restored and Daukes Hide, at least, completed in time for the planned Royal visit to go ahead as a fitting celebration of the 70th Anniversary of the Reserve and the Trust.

*

Father describes the great enjoyment Prince Philip always had from his visits to Cley, and like his father, Prince Charles has always taken a great interest in the Reserve. During his official visit he recalled how he had been sent to Cley as a child by Prince Philip to learn from my father something of the wildlife of the marsh. I was greatly honoured to be asked by HRH if he might in turn arrange a private visit for Prince William and Prince Harry, a visit that duly took place shortly afterwards.

Such events give one a great sense of continuity. But father's memoirs also remind us just how much times have changed. He grew up amongst the wildfowlers and gentleman gunners he so vividly describes, and though some would say he was a forthright man, I think he probably underplays the stresses and strains of dealing in those early years with deep-seated feeling towards new attitudes to conservation. And if there was local resentment it is, perhaps, not surprising. A way of life was disappearing, and a fundamental shift was taking place in the way that we approach places like this stretch of Norfolk coast.

The idea of managing wildlife habitat for any other than agricultural or sporting purposes was itself new, and I think father largely had to invent ways of doing it as he went along. With undue modesty, he made very little of the enormous fund of expert knowledge he built up over the years, and his own part in creating the Reserve that is enjoyed by so many people today.

The Good Old Days?

When, in January 1937, the late Sidney Long, who had founded the Norfolk Naturalists Trust in 1926, appointed me Warden of the Cley Nature Reserve, I reckoned I had landed the ideal job. I succeeded my grandfather, who had been the Warden for the previous ten years. The wages were £2 2*s* per week, out of which I was to pay 3*s* per week for rent of the newly-built Warden's house. At that time I was one of the better paid men of the village. An agricultural wage was only £1 11*s* 6*d* per week.

    From boyhood I'd been brought up with a love of shooting on the tideline and - though some people may find this hard to understand - a love of the birds who haunt the tideline. As a boy, I suppose the highlight of my year was the arrival at Cley during the migration periods of the bird collectors known as the Gentlemen Gunners. I'd better explain about them, for a start.

    The drill of a Gentleman Gunner was as follows. About a fortnight before September 1st, Rosson, the Norwich gunsmith delivered to certain regulars a thousand cartridges, usually a mixture of ten shot and fives. Beer and rum were also ordered, and usually a few beers were carted to the shore and hidden in some convenient rabbit hole, as a kind of reserve in case the Gentlemen Gunners had to walk the bushes and felt thirsty.

    The season for waders opened on September 1st, though there would have been sporadic shooting at duck since August 1st. The night before the season opened, *The George* and *The White Horse* in Blakeney filled up with the shooters and their families. The henchmen or boatmen met their employers to discuss operations and starting times for the morning, which were naturally affected by the tide. For the wealthy visitors, the shooting started at a civilised hour after breakfast. They were rowed down (tide permitting) to a boat moored at some favoured place on a flight-line.

The local wildfowlers started shooting long before that. By first light, around 5 am, they were lined out across the muds or hidden in the bushes at Rat Hill, Cart Road or Green Leaf Creek. Often - at least so it seems in my recollection - it was one of those fine autumn mornings, still, warm and silent, with a sort of velvety darkness, relieved only by the metallic sheen of water whispering over the muds. Before first light, the only sounds were the sucking noises of clams and skittering of gilly crabs and, over it all, the murmuring of the sea.

With first light came pandemonium, a regular barrage obliterating the soft piping and whistling of countless wading birds. It usually started with a single shot, the rolling crash rending the silence. For a moment there would be a hush and then a babble of bird noises, curlew squawking, redshank screaming, dunlin and ringed plover piping, and above all a mad rush of wings. Guns were soon going off all over the muds and marshes, muzzle-loaders booming, light twelves or twenties cracking or ringing, and boys' 'four tens' popping. In the confusion one thing was certain: few birds were killed, though many were frightened. The fusillade continued without diminishing until about 7.30 am by which time most of the local fowlers had fired off their ammunition or had to be off home to get ready for the day's work.

There was then a pause until the Gentlemen visitors arrived with their boatmen. There were usually five or six groups scattered over the muds. Then the really accurate shooting started. A great many waders were killed. Anything that moved was shot in the hope that it would prove to be a rare specimen. My father was henchman to one of these Gentlemen Gunners, a London solicitor named Frank Izod Richards, who employed him for the month of September at the then princely sum of 10*s* per day.

Before the first world war, Mr Richards was perhaps the best known collector and never missed a season on the Norfolk coast. Most

CLEY MARSH AND ITS BIRDS

Septembers he hired the old fishing smack *Britannia* and anchored her in a favourable position off Blakeney Point. Many a rare bird has been shot from her decks. Richards himself shot a fine adult red-breasted fly-catcher while perched on the bulwarks of the ship and a honey buzzard was downed with an 8-bore from the deck. My father became Izod Richards' henchman in the latter part of his collecting days. It was Mr Richards who gave me my first lessons in wader identification. He used to say that he had to live in London, for his sins. When staying at Cley he often used to lift his glass of beer in thanks-giving and say to my father: 'Billy, let us pray.' After a hard day's work shooting in the harbour, he would send his minions out after dark hunting for moths. Eventually he made a marvellous collection of British birds and moths. In it were waders in all stages of plumage. He was collecting, mind you, in the days when there weren't any affective protection laws, so that birds could be shot in their handsome spring plumage, as well as at all stages in between.

It was my duty as a schoolboy, for 2*s* a week, to carry the beer and the cartridges down to Mr Richards' boat before going to school and to bring back the empty beer bottles and any unwanted waders after school. These waders made excellent pies and provided a welcome contribution to my mother's larder. I sometimes wonder what some of the bird-lovers and watchers of today might think, when I say that of all the birds that were eaten by families such as mine, there is none to compare, in my opinion, with the lapwing or green plover. Plover pie was a real treat. The same green plover is today a protected bird. I often think it is the golden plover that should be protected. It is far less numerous when it visits Britain in winter than its green relative. The Gentlemen Gunners spared neither green, nor golden nor, for that matter, any other plover, including grey.

The gunner who will always be remembered as the most successful and scientific of the collectors was the late E.C. Arnold. For more than fifty years, he spent every September at Cley and eventually became the owner of an area east of the north end of the East Bank which now bears his name - Arnold's Marsh. I shall refer to it many times when writing about the present Cley Reserve.

When I first became Warden of Cley, E.C. Arnold used to sit in a boat in the middle of this area and shoot at every uncommon wader that passed. Arnold was a former headmaster of Eastbourne College. He sometimes brought with him three or four boys who were keen on birds and shooting. These were known locally as 'Arnold's greyhounds', probably because they were pretty quick at retrieving and flushing things from the bushes. Arnold himself was an excellent shot, especially in his younger days, and a good sportsman. He wrote several first-class outdoor books. His first, *A Bird Collector's Medley* became very popular and went into several editions. The last book, published in 1946, was *Memories of Cley*. I'm glad to say that I have a signed copy.

I recall Arnold hesitating to shoot one bird because he judged it to be a common species. His helper at that time was a wildfowler, Ted Ramm, son-in-law of the local taxidermist, no less than H.N. Pashley himself, author of *The Birds of Cley*. Ramm decided to shoot the bird in question himself. It proved to be a Pallas warbler which had probably flown from Siberia. It cost Arnold more than a mere trifle to get this rarity back from Ramm. The regrettable custom of shooting first and checking after was, I am afraid, the general practice. I have often seen a bucket filled with the more common migrants such as robins and redstarts, rejects from a Gentlemen Gunner's bag. The saying in those days was: 'What's hit is history. What's missed is mystery.' Ramm's random shot certainly solved the mystery of one rare bird.

Just occasionally, some protectionist tried to take a hand, especially if the villain was a local and not a Gentleman Gunner. Pashley states that a pair of roseate terns was shot by a lad in Blakeney Harbour in 1896, on June 24th. You'll learn who the lad grew up to be later in this book. Unexpectedly, he was prosecuted by the Society for the Prevention of Cruelty to Animals. He was convicted and fined, with costs, the sum of 23*s* 6*d*. Pashley himself paid the fine to save the boy from going to prison for seven days. The case had taken six months to come before the court. The chairman of the magistrates made it pretty warm for the Inspector of the RSPCA who prosecuted, saying that 'to let this case hang over the lad's head for six months may be law, but it's certainly not justice.'

I had often heard my father talk of the sandgrouse invasion referred to in Pashley's *The Birds of Cley*. It seems to me that the indiscriminate shooting that occurred at that time was largely responsible for the Bird

Protection Act of 1889. Thirty three specimens of sandgrouse passed through Pashley's hands for setting up. The first of these was seen by a landowner in the Cley area, a Mr W. Monement, and the last taken in the area on January 14th 1889. The sandgrouse were obviously found on the farms more than the free shooting areas of the marsh and foreshore, as the names of farmers and landowners are mentioned by Pashley more frequently than those of local wildfowlers. The Protection Act, passed in the summer of 1889, did not deter the collectors to any great extent and Pashley's book records considerable numbers of rarities that were taken to him to preserve and mount almost every month of the year. He instances a fine old male osprey that was brought to him on May 15th 1889.

Arthur Patterson, the naturalist author from Breydon - I shall have more to say about him later - claims in one of his books that the collecting of skins started at Breydon many years before it began at Cley. Pashley states that the first collectors who found Cley to be a Mecca for rare birds were two doctors, F.D. and G.E. Power.

The Power brothers discovered that the autumn migration of such birds as bluethroats and red-breasted fly-catchers, when leaving their northerly breeding grounds and returning along the western edge of the Continent, could be caught by a contrary wind and blown off course to the Norfolk coast. The Shingle Ridge from Cley to Blakeney Point is still famous for these tiny migrants, together with the even smaller goldcrests and firecrests, seeking shelter in the bushes that grow along the landward side of the beach from Cley to the Long Hills on Blakeney Point.

The two Power doctors both had practices in London. They engaged as their boatman a local wildfowler, 'Bloke' Brett, of whom more in a moment. Brett accompanied them on their collecting trips. With the help of his keen eyes, they were soon among the unusual bird visitors. They and those that followed in their footsteps soon realised that unless weather conditions were right there wouldn't be a bluethroat or fly-catcher in sight. With the help of such as Brett, the early collectors learned that an east wind and a mist at autumn migration was the ideal combination. To this day, such conditions are still referred to as 'a bluethroat morning'.

The Power brothers were followed by E.C. Arnold, F.I. Richards, C.D. Borrer and many others. The Gentlemen Gunners were somewhat like egg-collectors who only value a beautifully marked clutch of falcon's eggs if they take them from the nest personally. If a rare bird was found by one of the local wildfowlers, he usually went to a well-known collector and tipped him off so that the latter could shoot it himself. Some of them would have nothing in their collections that hadn't fallen to their own guns. By giving this kind of information, the wildfowlers usually got a better tip.

Looking at their activities from a modern conservationist view-point, there's no doubt the collectors did some dreadful things. All bluethroats were as eagerly sought after with guns as they are today with field-glasses. Many met an untimely end. According to old records, at least as many were shot then as are recorded today.

The first record for Norfolk of a yellow-breasted bunting was shot by E.C. Arnold on September 21st 1905, and the first desert wheatear for Norfolk (and the second for Great Britain) was killed by M. Catling on October 31st 1907.

The menace of the collectors went on right up until my own day as Warden, as the following story illustrates. I was delighted in my first year as Warden to find a bittern's nest at Cley within two hundred yards of my cottage. The nest contained four eggs. I at once telephoned Dr Sidney Long in Norwich, the Chairman of the Norfolk Naturalists Trust. He asked if I was sure of my facts. Could it perhaps be a pheasant's nest? I replied that it was a bittern that rose from the nest, well understanding his doubt, as the eggs of a bittern are very similar to a pheasant's in colour and size. Dr Long arrived at Cley in the shortest possible time it took to get from Norwich to confirm my discovery.

Living at Cley when the first bittern bred was that notable collector, C.D. Borrer. I knew that he had never 'got' his bittern and that our birds were therefore in danger. So I went to his house and told him that I had found this nest and I would not tolerate any interference with it. I knew that the parent bird, while catching food, would be very vulnerable. He promised me that he would leave them entirely alone for that year and he kept his word. After completing my war service I found he had got his bittern. He had promised to give his 16-bore gun to whoever could help him collect his specimen. I found a young fellow with the gun in question when resuming my Wardenship after the war.

Borrer, who turned out to be the last of the Gentlemen Gunners, stopped at nothing to get his quarry. I well remember a little egret appearing on the Cley Reserve. He tried every trick he could think of to get this bird, despite the fact that the shooting season had been over two months since. Every morning I met him at dawn with his loaded gun, and told him that he had no chance of getting that bird. These hardened collectors met fines with indifference. He told me once: 'There'll come a dawn, maybe, when you'll oversleep!' I never did.

Mr Borrer, who had settled in Cley at the Old Manor House, died in December 1961, and left his collection of birds, all of which had fallen to his own gun, to Cambridge University. The last addition to his collection, as far as I was aware, was an American pectoral sandpiper. It was a very tame bird and frequently fed on property belonging to Mr Borrer, so you could say it didn't stand much chance. While myself and two others were trying to photograph the bird, it actually walked under the camera tripod. After the bird had disappeared for a few days it was seen by the late Dr B. Riviere in a taxidermist's shop in Norwich. The man who skinned it said there wasn't a mark on it. It was so tame it had probably been netted. Mr Borrer knew all the tricks of the trade. But in the end, he at least partly atoned by leaving all his bodies to science. Cambridge University must have been very pleased with his collection. He wrote many nature articles for local papers and magazines under the name 'Sea Pie', and in one of these he left a fitting epitaph for the collectors:

> Such were some of the Gentlemen Gunners and their Henchmen. They belonged to a race that has almost passed away, like may other denizens of the swamps and marshes. They may become extinct, like many butterflies and birds.

And, of course, the keen and expert wildfowlers continued to haunt the coast, at least up until the mid 'Thirties. But how could those who foretold financial disaster have foreseen the present boom in ornithology and bird-watching? Thankfully, the marshes today are haunted by the binocular fraternity for all twelve months of the year and they bring far greater prosperity than the Gentlemen Gunners ever dreamed of.

The Old-Time Wildfowlers

Although my parents came from Cley, I was born some two miles distant in Blakeney, and it was there that I grew up and lived amongst some of the greatest wildfowlers who ever handled a gun.

There is little record of these early wildfowlers at Cley and would be even less but for H.N. Pashley. There was at that time a resident taxidermist in almost every town and village. I have my doubts whether any was busier or more skilful than H.N. Pashley, the resident taxidermist of Cley. Today, Pashley is best remembered for his *The Birds of Cley*, published in 1925. His diaries are full of references that help to reconstruct the early wildfowling and collecting days of the area. For instance, Pashley's diaries give some fascinating details about the old wildfowlers who helped the earliest of the Gentlemen Gunners. Two such, Moy and Pigott, lived in Salthouse, the village just a mile east of Cley. Moy claimed that he was the last person to collect avocets' eggs at Salthouse. He swore that the local gunners used to empty their muzzle-loaders into the avocet colony as they came home from shooting. Moy himself collected avocet eggs as a lad, so that his mother could make cakes with them!

The other old-timer from Salthouse was Gabriel Pigott, a big man with a flowing white beard. He lived to be nearly one hundred and during his fowling days had been credited with shooting more than one white-tailed sea eagle. They must have been much more common than now as I have seen only two during my entire lifetime on the Norfolk coast.

Pashley also mentions Gam Sturgess and another fowler who collected avocet eggs on Salthouse Broads. Professional fowling probably started with the coming of rail transport. This brought in visitors, at the same time causing a decline in the shipping trade. Records show that smuggling also declined and locals were in need of a new occupation, admittedly precarious, but capable of providing a living.

The tools of the early wildfowlers were muzzle-loaders either used from the shoulder or from a punt. The guns were long-barrelled with flint or percussion ignition. The shoulder gun was anything from 16 to 8 bore with sizes in between. It was possible to have a 13-bore muzzle-loader, because the barrels were made all sizes. The eights were massive devices of about fourteen pounds with four-foot barrels, and the twelves were not much smaller or lighter. Using these long-barrelled guns had its dangers, such as the muzzle getting choked with mud or snow, forgetting to take the ram-rod out of the barrel after loading, or sticking two charges down the barrel by mistake.

Gam Sturgess, Hugh Arthur Bishop, the Long brothers, Ted Buck, the Brett brothers and the other Bishops were all professional wildfowlers who worked the Harbour from Salthouse Broads to the East Hills of Wells. In the 'Seventies it was still possible to get a punt gun through to the Salthouse Broads from the main Harbour. Before the passing of the Forearms Act of 1884, few but the professional fowlers carried a gun, but after this guns and licences proliferated. Parties came down from nearby towns and blazed away at everything that moved. Colonel Peter Hawker referred to them as 'Tit Shooters', because they'd shoot at anything . Fortunately they did not spend much of their time on the Harbour during the winter months when the birds were there in big numbers. Cold wildfowling weather usually sent them home.

Hugh Arthur Bishop's name crops up in all records of fishing and wildfowling in Blakeney Harbour. I never knew him as he died before I was born and I am certain he was no relative. Certainly he was a great fowler and a great gentleman. He was the son of a Rector of Cley, who left him moderately wealthy. Unfortunately he lost his money and his wife at about the same time and for a while everything went wrong for him. He had been a seaman in his youth and had done a lot of oystering. He had shot for the collectors and had taken an osprey and a white stork and a few rare warblers. So when he lost his money he was well equipped to earn his living on the foreshore.

In general, Bishop lived the life of a professional fisherman, collector of skins and fowler. He had been known to throw a live cartridge into the bar fire at *The George and Dragon* in Cley, to see the locals move out in a hurry. He could tell a good story with the best of them. One of his favourites concerned the cleaning of his muzzle-loading gun. The nipple-hole was foul so he decided to clear it by firing the gun up the chimney. There was a really glorious bang as he'd left the ramrod in. As he pulled the gun out of the chimney there was a strange rumbling and bumping. Down the chimney came four duck neatly speared on the ramrod. Their feathers had been scraped off on the brickwork, the down singed off by the fire. The ramrod lodged across the fireplace just at the right height to act as a spit and roast them.

He spent the last years of his life fishing and fowling for his own amusement. This was the period when he ruptured himself hauling a heavy boat up the beach. When no medical aids were forthcoming, he used a barrel-hoop as a truss.

In October 1906, he was seen by a local fowler rowing out of the Harbour to catch mackerel. Actually, according to the wildfowler Ted Ramm, he was off over the bar to bag an eider drake that had been seen there, probably to sell to a collector. He took his crab-boat out on the ebb, single-handed, in spite of being told that it was unwise to go over the bar that day. He was never seen alive again and his body was picked up by Curly Catlin ten days later.

They were a grand bunch of fellows, those old gunners, and most of them possessed a keen sense of humour which enabled them to weather some pretty hard living conditions.

One family, especially, stands out in my mind, the Long family. Longs are still gunning on our coast, to this day. When I was growing up, this family consisted of eight boys and three girls but the Longs were active at all periods of my career. Three of them were extremely so just after the Second World War.

Each of these had the same Christian name - William. The eldest, Old Will, was an uncle to the eight boys. So was Middle Will. Young Will was a son of Middle Will. Old Will was still firing his punt gun when he was seventy-four years old. Middle Will, as I shall relate, had his forearm blown off in a punt gun accident, but he carried on punting and taught himself to row using two oars with one hand. During the winter the fowlers and their families kept themselves going on duck and it was the normal thing for them to have a duck each for a meal.

Most of the Long brothers had a wonderful sense of humour. George, the second eldest, emigrated to New Zealand and for many years worked on a sheep farm before returning to Blakeney to take up the trade of his brothers. He had acquired the nickname 'Wongie' whilst abroad and the name stuck for the rest of his life. His humorous stories are now legendary among those who knew him, and I would like to put on record one or two of them.

He had a dog, a labrador called Caesar, of which he was very fond. He would talk to it as if it were human. He had a marvellous understanding with this dog. One late afternoon during a very hard spell of frost, the dog looked up at his master and whimpered to go out for the evening duck flight. George says himself he was rather reluctant to go but the dog persisted, so he gathered his gun and cartridges and set out for what was known as the East Muds. It was an excellent feeding ground for wigeon since it was covered with *Zostera marina*, sometimes called eel grass, which wigeon love.

George and his dog crouched in one of the dykes. The temperature was well below freezing point and it was not long before the dog whimpered and gave the impression it had had enough and wanted to return home. George wasn't having any. 'It's your damn fault we're out here at all, when we both could have been sitting beside a nice warm fire. I'm going to make you sit there till your backside freezes to the mud.' I don't suppose he did. George didn't want his own backside frozen, so they both probably spent the rest of the night roasting by a cosy fire.

I asked George one morning how he had got on during the previous evening's flight. He said he was much amused by some character who had taken up position near him, to try to attract the wigeon by what he thought was an imitation of the drake's whistling call. This merely

THE OLD-TIME WILDFOWLERS

scared the birds off. 'No wonder,' said George, 'he sounded like a nanny goat piddling on a corrugated iron roof.'

Out of the shooting season, the locals had other strings to their bows. Most of them were inshore shell fishermen with their own areas in Blakeney Harbour where they laid down young mussels to grow to edible size. There were various places where the young mussels could be gathered for this purpose. One of these was Morston Cockle Strand. If these immature mussels were not collected and were allowed to grow old before they were cultivated, their growth was retarded and they became useless for eating. George was inspecting some of these poor quality mussels one morning when a friend asked him what he thought of them. 'I reckon,' George said, 'these mussels have been there since Julius Caesar was a Lance Corporal.'

These young seed mussels were also brought into Blakeney Harbour from the mussel scaups which flourished in the Wash. Among the boat crews engaged in this work were some real characters. The youngest member of a boat crew bringing mussels into Blakeney Harbour, being ordered to 'make the tea' approached the boiling kettle, only to be told by his uncle Sammy, 'Don't do anything with that kettle for a few more minutes.' The youth, rather mystified at this request, sat down to wait and was astonished to see his uncle lift the lid of the kettle and remove a large goose egg out of the boiling water. The farmyard condition in which the egg had originally been placed in the water was still so clearly evident that the boy decided he didn't want any tea!

Yet another of the old generation of wild fowlers was Joe Mitchell, a bricklayer by trade and almost stone deaf. For a wildfowler, this is a severe handicap as one often hears duck before seeing them in the fading light. However, Joe had the eyesight of an eagle and would always return from a duck flight with more than his share. In his spare time he acted as keeper to the then manager of the Blakeney Hotel, a Captain Barker. I became involved with Joe in his role as part-time keeper in a dispute over the ownership of a certain pair of mallard. I said that I had shot them on public ground and Joe swore I had shot them on Captain Barker's land. This incident occurred just before my application for the Warden's job at Cley. Since everyone knows everyone else's business where such matters are concerned, I wasn't expecting the affair to stand much in my favour. So, much to my surprise, when I went for the interview with the late Dr Long, then Secretary of the Norfolk Naturalists Trust, I was informed that this self-same hotel manager, Captain Barker, had given me an excellent testimonial. This, of course, I could hardly believe and said so. Dr Long looked at me a minute or two and then came out with the following. 'Captain Barker says that you're the biggest poacher in Blakeney, so he reckons you should make an excellent keeper.' There's a lot in that, I thought, gratefully accepting the job.

All told, Captain Barker had a bit of a rough time. He was a very keen gardener and carried off most of the prizes at the annual flower show. Another of the Long tribe, Matty, decided it was time to put a stop to this. The night before the show, he paid a visit to Barker's garden and helped himself to the pick of the produce. The following day it was Matty who carried off most of the prizes. Captain Barker was somewhat mystified by this. Afterwards he said to Matty: 'I didn't know you were a gardener or even that you had a garden.' 'I've just taken it up,' said Matty, but he didn't say (not then, anyway!) where he'd taken it up from.

In those days, the talk in the bar of the local was always of guns and what was shot rather than of binoculars and cameras and what had been seen, as it is today. Notable shots were recorded. A local punt-gunner claimed to have killed in three shots 120 knot, eight shelduck and twenty-seven brent geese!

On February 17th 1900, George Long and sons of Blakeney, together with Tom Cringle of Wells, lined their punt-guns up together and fired into a very big flock of knot. From 80 yards they picked up 603 knot, nine redshanks and six dunlin. I can well imagine that many more were wounded, to be eaten by predators later.

One of my favourite tales told by these old gunners came from an old Stiffkey wildfowler, who swore that while loading his 12-bore muzzle-loader, his ramrod got stuck in the barrel just as a skein of geese passed within gunshot. He aimed and pulled the trigger. The ramrod passed through five of the geese which fell on a covey of partridges, killing five of them. The recoil was naturally greater than normal, knocking him to the ground, so that he fell on a hare that had been crouching in the grass and killed it. He got such a fright that he toppled into a dyke. When he pulled himself out, his two long rubber boots were full of eels. He considered that this was the most profitable shot he ever made and I daresay he was right, at that.

Coastal wildfowlers are not noted for their care with guns, or anyway for care of their guns. The rough salty conditions in which they shoot aren't greatly in favour of loving gun maintenance. Marine mud doesn't help, especially when muzzles are accidentally stuck into it when crossing a gutter or creek. All told, I am amazed that there are not more accidents on the saltings with guns. We certainly had our share in our small quarter of Norfolk.

At the turn of the century, Bloke Brett of Blakeney - already referred to as a henchman to the Power brothers - had an arm blown off. The accident that cost him one of his hands and part of his wrist happened when he was quite a young man. He fell into a snowdrift while stalking a bunch of teal that had dropped into the River Glaven. While trying to get his old muzzle-loader out of the drift, the barrel - which was choked with snow - exploded, blowing his hand and wrist to pieces. It was said that he carried his gun home. After this, he had an iron hook attached to the stump of his arm and used to say it was nearly as useful as a hand. He could still fire his gun from his shoulder, steadying the barrel with his hook. He was reputed to be a first-class shot and used a large single barrelled 4-bore which he had painted white so as not to be conspicuous in snowy or moonlight conditions. Off-white, or 'kittiwake grey', incidentally, is the colour favoured by punt-gunners for making their guns and punts inconspicuous to fowl. He claimed formidable feats with this gun, saying that after firing into a large flock of dunlin, he picked up ninety-nine. It was a subject of deep regret that he didn't find his hundredth bird. Like many of these old wildfowlers, he was a very strong and hard man but didn't look after himself. There are men still living who can remember him standing in front of the fire in *The George* bar drying himself, with a cloud of steam coming from his wet clothes. In later years he suffered with severe rheumatism.

Another sad accident occurred in the early 1930s. A wildfowler named Priney Hagan paused to speak to a colleague walking along the top of a bank, strangely another of the Brett family. Whilst talking, he stood his gun down with the stock on the ground while holding it with his fingers over the top of the barrels which were angled towards Harry Brett. Brett's dog, jumping up at Hagan, caught its paw on Hagan's trigger. The gun discharged, killing poor Harry. A broken trigger-guard was to blame this time. It hadn't been replaced on Hagan's gun.

A few years later, the early dawn found William Long of Blakeney - this was Middle Will, whom I've already mentioned - out in his boat loading his punt-gun in preparation for some duck-shooting. It might have been the dim light of the morning or just plain carelessness, but he failed to ensure that the heavy breech block was safely home and locked. I saw him that morning running as fast as he could towards the village with the shattered remains of his forearm bundled up in his blood-soaked coat. If pressed, he would relate the gruesome detail of how he trimmed up the stump of his arm. However, he must have done a good job. It was not long before he was punting again, having taught himself to handle two oars with his remaining hand.

A regular February feature was the organised hare shoot. All sorts and varieties of local sportsmen took part. Some of the firearms brought to these shoots should have been pensioned off years before. The gunners would pile into any available transport. Some of the conveyances were as rickety as the guns. In one trailer sat an aged agricultural hand clutching a decrepit old gun with barrels mercifully, and probably largely by chance, pointing at the canvas roof. When the trailer started, it gave the gun a slight jar, releasing the defective trigger sear so that the gun discharged, blowing a great hole in the roof. The old chap was not greatly perturbed, merely commenting: ' That's a b----r. The same thing happened last week.'

At least five per cent of the guns used by local fowlers were unserviceable, to say the least. It was quite the thing to have an elastic band around the stock to hold the top-lever, which keeps the gun closed, in place; or for the stock to be bound up with copper wire if it was broken or cracked. If a hole had rusted through the barrels, the normal practice was to solder a piece of razorblade over it. After World War II, even the locals had come to appreciate the dangerous qualities of firearms. Most of these old guns became collectors' pieces and were thankfully withdrawn from service and hung on the wall.

Up to the early 'Thirties there were at least fifty punt-gunners still operating on the north Norfolk coast. I well remember the pride of one of this hardy race of sportsmen telling how he had glided past a redshank sitting on the edge of Morston Creek without disturbing it, and then getting a shot at a party of wigeon 200 yards down the creek. He was much more pleased with his feat in passing the ever-alert wader than bagging a number of ducks. Punt-gunning is by far the most difficult form of wildfowling. Its lessons have to be learned in the hard school of experience.

With the passing of the Gentlemen Gunners and the mysterious disappearance of the flat fish in the mid 'Twenties, especially the flounders, in and around Blakeney Harbour, the livelihood of the local wildfowlers and fishermen began to suffer. At the same time, the numbers of terns breeding in the area was increasing rapidly. Naturally, they were blamed for the shortage of fish. So the Ministry of Agriculture and Fisheries gave permission for a number of terns to be shot and sent to the Yorkshire Museum for analysis of the food found in them. This was done in the breeding season of 1925.

The shooting of the terns was to be carried out by my father in conjunction with Mr R. Pinchen, who at that time was the Warden of Blakeney Point. A total of forty-eight common terns, nine sandwich terns and six little terns were shot and sent off. I well remember my father pouring a teaspoonful of methylated spirits down each bird's gullet, then plugging their throats with cotton wool for the better preservation of whatever they had eaten. The Museum scientists found that the terns were in no way to blame for the shortage of fish and the material loss to the fishermen. It was soon realised that the revenue lost by these men could be regained by taking numbers of visitors over to Blakeney Point to see the tern colonies.

This state of affairs went on for a few years, and then the blame for the shortage of fish was placed on the increasing numbers of common seals. Again, the Ministry tried to help and offered 10s (50 pence) for the snout of each seal shot. The snout had to be shown to a Ministry official. It soon became evident that this was not a good idea. The carcasses of the seals began to wash ashore on to the beaches and cause pollution. The story of the terns was repeated. Today, the loss in fishing is made up by ferrying hundreds of visitors to see the seals on the Blakeney sand banks.

Among the many distinguished visitors to the Blakeney area of the Norfolk coast was the late Sir Henry Birkin of motor racing fame, one of the great Bentley drivers of the 'Thirties. He was held in great affection by all the locals to whom he was known as 'Tim' and much respected as a keen and very able wildfowler.

On one occasion, when he was taking part in a twenty-four-hour endurance race on the famous Brooklands race track in Surrey, he arranged for a party of locals to travel by coach to London and from there to Brooklands, to watch the race. For some of the party this was the first time they had been outside Norfolk. It was suggested they should all wear civilised dress including, for the first time in many of their lives, a necktie. My father was one of the party. I well remember the uproar caused by my mother when she insisted on putting a tie around father's neck.

The party was away for five days. On his return, my father's first words to my mother were: 'Sarah, will you take this damn thing off. I've had it on all the week. I knew if I took it off, I'd never get it on again.' Incidentally, Sir Henry won the race.

At the time of writing this there is only one punt-gunner left on this part of the Norfolk coast, Stratton Long, the eldest son of the boy who was prosecuted for shooting roseate terns in 1896, referred to in another chapter. Stratton is the right sort. For him, a successful approach stalk is more important than the final shot.

As the years passed, the fowling grew less good. There was a great period of abundance in the early 'Twenties, due to the resting of the breeding grounds during the 1914-1918 War and the flooding of the Cley Marshes and the Glaven Valley in 1921. Already, by the middle of the 'Thirties, fowling was beginning to decline. For one thing, more people had guns. For another, the motor car made areas like Cley accessible to keen fowlers in the cities. In the 'Thirties, when duck shooting started on August 1st, the season literally began with a bang that reminded one of the heyday of the Gentlemen Gunners. Cartridges were cheap. Everything was shot at, even if very little was actually killed. After the first two days, few took the trouble to go out at morning and evening flight. As usual things found their own level. Only the hard core stuck it out when the weather got rough.

The Highs and Catlins in Blakeney, the Longs and Bishops and the Holmans of Salthouse were among the real and possibly the only regulars. By 1939, the end of North Norfolk wildfowling as it was once known was fast approaching. In the six years that followed, the end was sadly reached for many of the young men who would have carried on. A shorter shooting season, fewer birds and a different channel of thought towards conservation and ornithology ended the old pattern.

During the war years some casual fowling was done by the older men who remained. The Royal Observer Corps had cleverly erected a lookout post for enemy aircraft on the flight line for duck passing between the Cley Marshes and Blakeney Harbour. I suspect they identified more mallard than Heinkels. The flack they sent up was more 12-bore than ack-ack gun. It must have helped their meat ration quite a bit. Good luck to them! Whenever I got a spot of winter leave, I took full advantage of the same facility to help out my wife and children's larder.

Arriving home for Christmas in 1941, I was greeted with the news that we should perhaps have to kill a backyard hen if we were to have a fowl on the Christmas dinner table. Instead, I found five cartridges in the house and, as it was getting dark, set out on a little maraud. Within five minutes, a fine hare jumped from its seat and was neatly bowled over. A short stroll and two pheasants were added. Within the next 100 yards I downed two more pheasants. I cannot think that I had bagged five more acceptable additions to the larder in my whole life. My joy was somewhat diluted when the local bobby stopped me to ask if I had a Game Licence. I told him that as I didn't need a licence to fire a 12-pounder gun at German E boats while mine-sweeping between Sheerness and Dover, I didn't consider that I needed one to shoot pheasants. That was the end of that particular conversation.

After the war, a few young men tried to do some professional fowling but the restrictions imposed by the Wild Birds Protection Act and more general commonsense towards bird life had ended the free-for-all era along the coast. Many like myself, who were brought up amongst the collectors and 'tit-shooters', began to learn about telescopic lenses, Heligoland traps and tape recorders. There were many keen and expert naturalists visiting the area who were glad to pass on their own special expertise. I won't say we all became totally 'reformed' characters like Sir Peter Scott. Wildfowling was in our blood. Nevertheless we began to see the other side of the picture. Perhaps better than most, the expert hunter understands the messages and principles of conservation. The conversion, or anyway adaptation, to ornithology for such as myself was therefore not only easy but exciting.

The final passing of the day of the Gentlemen Gunners came in 1948 when Gilmour Richards, the son of one of the better-known old Collectors, dressed in thigh boots, tweeds, cap and sidebag, came down in September as his father had done for many years, and was taken down to Blakeney Harbour by my father to relive once again something which he knew his father and mine had enjoyed.

It was an era worth growing up in, and one which will never be repeated. I have no regrets for taking part in it and neither have I any regrets for seeing it come to an end. I still feel proud of killing all four in a skein of white-fronted geese with two shots and could now go to the spot where my first mallard fell. I am as proud of those early wildfowling feats as I was when I found and showed the late Dr Long our first bittern's nest in 1937.

Wildfowling is much more than just the shooting. To me it will always be the memory of incredible dawns when the whole sky to the East caught fire in gold and scarlet; the days when snow covered everywhere and ice floes floated in on the tide as it covered the muds; the nights when one suddenly caught sight of half a dozen wigeon silhouetted against the moon; and a successful shot. These were the things we wanted at that time and they were among the memories we treasure. Having had these experiences myself, I have and will always do my utmost to see that my sons and their sons have the chance to carry on the sport. Where in my younger days we shot as many as possible, the younger generation are content with a brace, and the relationship between conservation bodies and wildfowlers has never been better. There is room for both.

Most wildfowlers are good conservationists at heart. I fully understand their point of view. I am, as you might say, on both sides of the fence or perhaps both sides of the sea wall would be a more accurate description. After becoming Warden, I spent most of my time on the landward side of that frontier. But I shall never forget the magic of the sport I've enjoyed where the flowing tide meets the edge of the saltings. Let me try to describe one such occasion for you.

There is something magical about an evening flight on an open estuary like Blakeney Harbour. The mud flats are open to the North

Sea, the winds coming straight in from the icepack, blowing over no land since leaving Spitzbergen, and rarely less than Force Five. The sky has a steely, hard appearance which is reflected in the water-filled dykes and creeks. Out to sea, there is complete emptiness while to landward the higher ground lies crowned with dull patches of woodland where the pheasants are about to go up to roost for the night. The outlines of these woods are gently softened by the dusk. It is into this world, when conditions are right for an evening flight that one melts unobtrusively.

In warm, heavy kit and with gun under arm and shovel slung across your shoulders, you make your way, slipping and sliding over the mud, to where a few feathers or droppings show signs of habitation by duck. Laying the gun on the driest spot you can find, you dig yourself a shallow hole and line it with dry grass, gathered on your way down over the saltings. In this 'grave' one crouches, facing downwind, the direction you expect the duck to come in to feed, knowing full well that the hole in which you put your feet will be at least half full of water by the time the flight has ended!

The distant call of the curlew and the piping of other waders lend enchantment to your vigil. With the first glimpses of a star comes the sound of ducks' wings swishing overhead and passing peacefully out of range. You hope the next party will come lower as the light fails. Again the faint sound of swishing duck wings and your hand tightens on the gun. Within a split second there are fowl within a few yards of your head. Your first duck crumbles at your second shot and falls with a very satisfactory thump on the mud.

Partly for a chance to stretch your legs, you climb out of your 'gun-hole' as they were usually called, to pick up your duck. As you do so, the honking of geese attracts your attention. With skidding footsteps you hurry back to your hole, only to see the geese passing up inland well out of range to your right. After a further twenty minutes the flight is over. If you're lucky you may have two or three duck. With great satisfaction you make your way over the saltings towards the flickering lights of the village.

I was once asked to load at a big covert shoot day at Holkham by the late Earl of Leicester, for someone he termed 'a very important guest'. The gun concerned turned out to be Lord Wavell, one of the finest

Generals of the Second World War. During a pause between drives, he asked to define what, in my opinion, made a genuine wildfowler. After some thought, I told him that it was a man who faced the bitter winds and frost on the Norfolk coast, and who, returning wet through, frozen and empty-handed, immediately made plans to go out again the next night.

Lord Wavell expressed delight at this definition and told me that when he was Viceroy in India he was invited to shoot with the Heads of State. At these *battues*, the bags of duck ran into many hundreds and sometimes topped the thousand mark. The hides or butts were made very comfortable and one could order a whisky and soda. He said that he would have traded them all in for a chance to join me for an evening flight in Blakeney Harbour.

Local Relations

Before the Second World War and for many years after, the feelings of wildfowlers towards all conservation bodies were, to say the least, strong. The laws governing the free shooting of wildfowl were, perhaps wilfully, or occasionally in good faith and sheer ignorance, not understood.

As a youngster, I myself believed you could shoot a duck, simply because it was wildfowl and not game, anywhere. It was generally believed that the public had the right to shoot anywhere below the highwater mark and this included the foreshore.

In the 'Thirties, the shooting season for duck began on August 1st and ended on the last day of February. Later the season was curtailed on the foreshore, opening on August 12th and closing on February 20th. None of this made the situation any clearer to local gunners or the job of a Warden any easier, especially in the first years after World War II. Trespass, poaching and thoughtless behaviour seemed to be the natural reaction to wartime disciplines.

For many years, one of my most thankless tasks was to try to stop wildfowlers from shooting on the East Bank at Cley. My grandfather, the first Warden for the Norfolk Naturalists Trust, had been getting old for a few years before I took over. Naturally I took a stronger line and there was much bad feeling when I reported one or two of the locals to the Trust for illicit shooting.

The police were not keen to take action. So, for several years, the Trust tried to stop the trespassing gunners by writing letters threatening them with prosecution if they did not refrain from shooting on the Reserve in future. After this had gone on for a few years, some of the local fowlers decided to fight against the Trust's right to stop shooting on the East Bank. The Trust was able to prove damage and won its case. In 1954, the Protection of Birds Act was passed and a much clearer picture emerged of where one could legally shoot, namely on the foreshore as defined by the seaward side of the mean high tidemark. Mind you, this only applies where the foreshore is owned by the Crown, as most of it is. Today you have to be a member of the British Association for Shooting and Conservation (formerly WAGBI) even to shoot there, a far cry from the old free-for-all days. Nevertheless, supervision of this sort is an excellent thing. Wildfowling clubs control their members well and prevent the irresponsible types usually referred to as 'marsh cowboys' from damaging conditions for other fowlers and, more important, the fowl.

After the 1954 Act, a much more friendly atmosphere began to emerge and local gunners formed their own wildfowling club. The feeling between the Trust and local fowlers is better now than I ever dreamt possible twenty-five years ago.

We have had one or two very hard winter months lately, when very severe weather prevailed in Norfolk and other parts of the country. The Secretary of State for the Environment, in consultation with wildfowling and ornithological bodies, banned all shooting of wildfowl for periods of a fortnight at a time. It is a pleasure to record that many of our local wildfowlers gave up shooting willingly well before the ban was imposed and did not shoot that year on the foreshore even after the ban was lifted. They did this to give the duck a chance to recover before the breeding season. The local wildfowler's club bought a quarter of a ton of barley for the Warden at Cley to feed the duck on the Reserve.

Bringing Back the Lost Species

Over the past forty years many attempts have been made to lure back to Norfolk, to breed, some of the species that have forsaken us in the distant past. A variety of devices were used, not all were successful.

In the case of ruffs and reeves, just prior to the Second World War, some twenty reeves were imported from Holland by Dr Riviere. At that time, he was Honorary Treasurer of the Norfolk Naturalists Trust. We immobilised the birds by clipping the primaries of one wing. The initial operation proved ineffectual as the bird was still able to fly. On release, it lost no time heading off in an easterly direction, no doubt on its way back to Holland. It was obviously necessary for more extensive clipping to secure immobility. Thus treated, the next batch of birds in their enforced residence failed to produce a local colony. I have reason to believe this was partly due to a pair of shorteared owls nesting in the vicinity at the time. It was then decided to try to produce a lekking ground where the males display, similar to those I had seen in Holland a few years previously. Ruffs, the males of the species - females are called reeves - need to dance and display to each other in sufficient numbers and with sufficient intensity to work themselves up to breeding pitch. For various reasons, some unknown, the attempt failed also.

In 1964, I again visited Holland, this time to study the habitats of blacktailed godwits, avocets and black terns. I returned with quite a few ideas. In the case of black terns work was put in hand to construct rafts covered with wire netting and reed. These were located in places where it was known these birds regularly stay to rest and feed on their annual spring migrations. Sadly, however, only gulls made use of them as nesting sites.

However, not all our efforts were in vain. An attempt was made to manage the grazing to produce conditions similar to those in the meadows where we had seen blacktailed godwits breeding in Holland. Grazing was controlled in such a way that the grass was left just long enough for the birds to make their scrapes while still being able to look around whilst sitting. Within one years, two pairs of blacktailed godwits were on eggs.

With such encouragement, it was then decided to try to lure back the avocets, and, as I shall shortly describe, scrapes were made. As is well known, there is now a thriving colony of avocets at Cley. The lesson was there for all to see - get the habitat right and the nesting birds will follow.

When *Where to Watch Birds*, by John Gooders, appeared in 1967, it resulted in a very large increase at Cley of visiting bird-watchers. Gooders wrote: 'There can hardly be a serious bird-watcher in the country who has not made the pilgrimage to Cley; it has been the Mecca of ornithologists for the last 140 years. The East Bank at Cley is considered to be the best place in England to watch passage waders and to meet well-known bird-watchers.'

The East Bank overlooks a small saltwater area known as Arnold's Marsh. For such a limited area its record for rarities is second to none. The marsh is only slightly affected by the rise and fall of tides, but the shingle ridge to the north has encroached at least 80 yards in my lifetime. The marsh has therefore been shrinking and deteriorating fast as a breeding ground for waders.

It was with this in mind that I was anxious to create alternative feeding areas for waders on the Cley Reserve. When Arnold's Marsh was purchased by E.C. Arnold it was around 29 acres in extent. After the flood in 1953 the actual feeding area had shrunk to approximately half that size. On the death of Mr Arnold it was left to the National Trust but was to be managed by the Norfolk Naturalists Trust.

During the early 1960s, a local Army Training Camp made an effort to create an area similar to Arnold's Marsh to the south of Taylor's Hill but very little was achieved owing to limited time and unfavourable weather. However, everyone could see that the potential was there. In 1964, a small pool was made to attract waders, close to a new hide overlooking the Cley Reserve, approximately 400 yards to the west of the East Bank. The pool was not big enough to be effective. It was when discussing my plan to enlarge this pool with a keen ornithologist, Justin Carter, that he suggested I should start a fund in order to put my ideas into practice. He offered to start the fund off with a cheque for £100.

At the time we were fortunate to have a plant hire firm in the village owned and managed by Mr Peter Newland, a young man who was very keen on the preservation of wildlife and anxious to help in any way possible. That the work involved in making the new pools, or scrapes, on Cley marsh proceeded so efficiently during the next few years was largely due to Peter Newland's drivers, Alfred Painter and Stanley Moore, who were keen ornithologists and dedicated to the preservation of wildlife themselves. The work began with the enlargement of the small pool in front of the new hide. It was apparent at once that we were on the right track. Waders flocked in to the new areas of exposed mud right under the wheels of the machines.

Other generous people came along with support for this new venture. Dr Robinson, Miss Luckett and Mr Bernard Simmonds offered to pay for two further scrapes. Miss Luckett also donated a new hide to overlook one of the new scrapes. The wife of Mr Bernard Simmonds, Mrs Irene Simmonds, donated a further hide. Many other people gave money towards this work. We were able to improve the north scrape and improve the control of water levels, so that there were always areas where waders and ducks could rest and feed.

From then on, visiting bird-watchers had a much more profitable and exciting time, viewing from the new hides over the scrapes. They weren't the only ones to benefit. The income of the Trust from the Cley Reserve increased by 25 per cent annually as a result of the extra permits bought to visit the hides. I am certain that had it not been for such habitat improvements, birds like the avocet and blacktailed godwit would not have been induced to return to breed in Norfolk again after a period of 150 years.

While we were improving conditions for rare waders, natural habitat was fast declining, or anyway altering, for the ducks and geese. This had, in fact, been happening over a long period, perhaps as much as forty years. When plans were being made for a proposed third London Airport on Maplin Sands, there was bitter opposition from the conservationists who claimed great areas of *Zostera marina*, or eel grass, the main food of wigeon and brent geese, would disappear, with disastrous results for these species. Forty years ago there were at least 50 to 60 acres of this same *Zostera* in Blakeney Harbour. Then a disease struck the *Zostera* beds of the North Atlantic coasts. Today, I doubt if there are 5 acres left and yet in winter there are just as many wigeon and decidedly more brent than in those earlier days. Up to 1,500 brent winter in the area today and are starting to make a nuisance of themselves by moving onto the farmers' winter wheat.*

Prior to 1964, the main resting place for wigeon was the lake in Holkham Park, but when all shooting ceased in that year on the Cley Reserve, these selfsame duck began to rest on the marsh in their thousands, reaching peak numbers during November. They began to graze on the short grass that grew after the cattle had been taken away in the autumn. Like the brent, they appear to have forgotten all about the vanished *Zostera*. At the present time there are very few wigeon resting or feeding on Holkham Lake. It just shows how adaptable wildfowl can be, given an alternative resting or feeding ground.

Where the *Zostera* grew in the old days in Blakeney Harbour, there is now a much coarser grass, chord grass or *Spartina maritima*. It has spread over three parts of the area that in my fowling days was open mud-flats. If this continues, as seems likely, the areas known as the East and West muds and the Little and Big Shingle Knoll will be just a memory as far as wildfowl are concerned. *Spartina* is quite unpalatable.

In the years preceding the Second World War, a great number of grey geese - the majority pinkfeet - regularly came to Blakeney Harbour and Wells, resting by day on the great expanse of sands between the two harbours, flighting inland to feed at night, and returning to rest at dawn the following morning. However, just prior to the Second World War, an anti-aircraft practice camp was built at Stiffkey. This overlooked the sands. The birds were disturbed during daylight hours and, having nowhere to rest in peace, left the area never to return.*

* The status of geese in the area has changed considerably since 1983 - see Checklist.

Canada geese were at this time beginning to increase at Cley. Twenty years ago the odd pair nested there. By 1980, approximately forty to fifty pairs were breeding. A winter population of about three hundred are seen feeding daily on the reserve with some thirty greylags.

When bitterns started to breed at Cley in 1937, I had the desire to study them as very little was known about them at that time and I had a unique opportunity to do so. There were very few rules and regulations regarding restrictions in visiting nests or controlling ringing of birds and I was able to purchase rings with my own name and address stamped on them.

In 1939 I ringed a young bittern at Cley and the following year it was knocked down by a lorry in Cheshire and taken to Manchester zoo where it was nursed back to health and later released. I had reason to believe that it returned to Cley.

Bittern are often referred to during the breeding season as pairs, but I have no evidence that they ever pair. It is thought by some that a pair needs 5 acres of reed beds to breed and that reeds must be 5 feet tall. This I have never found to be correct. It has been my experience that a male bird will dominate a 5 acre area but will often have more than one female in his area. I have found nests only a few feet apart in rushes less than 2 feet tall.

I have yet to see more than three young birds reared from one nest despite the fact that four and sometimes five eggs are laid. The hen starts to sit as soon as she has laid her first egg which means that by the time the last egg is due to hatch the eldest chick is hungry and, as the male bird has nothing to do with the rearing of the chicks, the female has to leave the nest to search for food. Leaving the nest results in the last eggs getting chilled, and even if more than three do hatch the youngest always seems to disappear and I have always had my suspicions that it has been eaten by the older chicks.

The late Lord Alanbrooke and R.P. Bagnall-Oakeley, both of whom were very eminent photographers of wild life, spent many hours in hides overlooking bitterns' nests and it was found that the young are rarely if ever fed more than three times in one day. Despite this they grow rapidly and when visiting a nest when the young had recently been fed I have witnessed a nine day old bittern chick disgorge a complete half-grown moorhen. Nothing comes amiss to a bittern in the way of food; they will eat almost anything, and I am certain that they take the eggs and young of many reed nesting birds.

When in Iceland in 1942, a friend of mine was returning home to England and expressed the desire to film a bittern at the nest during the following breeding season. The advice I gave him was to walk through the reed beds in a north westerly direction for a quarter of a mile from my hut. At that moment I had no idea whether the birds had returned to nest. He thought that I was pulling his leg, but on my return he told me that I had been 5 yards out as he had found a nest at 435 yards which goes to prove that bitterns will return to almost the same spot to breed year after year.

These birds suffer badly in severe winters, and during the hard frosts in 1963 it was estimated that 95 per cent of bitterns at Cley were wiped out. Efforts to feed them were made by scattering sprats in among the reed beds where they were thought to be, but there were many other animals and birds that were in the same state and I had my doubts whether they found the food while it was still palatable.

A few days later I found a bittern in the reeds that was so weak it could not move. It did manage to peck me but nevertheless I carried it home and it soon fed on sprats whilst I sat and watched.

I was wondering what to do with this bird in the end, when I remembered that Lord Buxton already had one injured bittern in a marshland enclosure at his home at Stanstead. His bird had collided with a lorry in Broadland and broken its beak. A passer-by had rescued it and looked after it - he said that it used to sit under his television set in the living room - and then he took it to Ted Piggin, the keeper at Hickling. Since the bird could not fend for itself with a broken beak, Ted handed it over for safety to the Buxton reserve. I never realised that my bittern would before long help to make history.

Lord Buxton had always been determined to obtain film of a bittern booming for the *Survival* series, and had even let it be passed around that there would be £1,000 for the first footage of a booming bittern. He was always a bit dubious (as I was) of biologists and bird experts who claimed to describe how bitterns boom. All their descriptions were different. So it was a lucky accident for ornithologists that he suddenly finished up with two bitterns (but not necessarily 'a pair') in a beautiful enclosed area next to an old boat house within five minutes of his house, from which it was possible to observe every move through slits in the boarded walls.

The bitterns settled down together very well for a year. Then incredibly, when Lord Buxton was taking dogs for a walk round the park at 7 am, he suddenly heard a bittern cough. Not exactly a boom, but unmistakably a cough, the same that comes before the boom. He and a friend ran several hundred yards to get into a better position, and then in 'unbelievable excitement' as he called it, they actually heard a bittern boom at Stanstead, presumably for the first time in history.

Lord Buxton wrote to me as follows:

> Within the hour I was sitting in the boat house watching a bittern boom - the very thing I had yearned to see for decades. But it was quite a shock. All the famous descriptions by experts were proved phoney. Quite honestly I was a bit embarrassed at first, because the bittern looked as if it was blowing off through its backside. This seemed rather a tawdry climax to the greatest discovery on earth and I wondered in what language I was going to announce it to the world!

But it became apparent that the bittern was in fact sucking in air and blowing up its air sack and then expelling it with a resonant boom, like a Kori Bustard in Africa; the whole body shook and shuddered, but mercifully it was not in fact blowing off at the back.

The booming bittern had its head and beak downwards as if it was going to be sick, and the actual act of booming was similar to a dog retching. So spectacular and sensational was this affair - Lord Buxton described it as 'the greatest single event in my amateur ornithological experience' - that photographers Ted Eales and George Edwards were summoned within hours and the broken-beaked bittern had been filmed booming before the end of that very day, which was a Sunday. Ted said that when he went to report his success to his Lordship, he was in the middle of a fierce set of tennis, but insisted on Ted going back and filming it again to be on the safe side.

This unique film footage was eventually included in the special *Survival* film about Norfolk conservation entitled 'Norfolk in Trust'. It is the only film of a bittern booming and will probably be the last.

The reason for all the excitement was that nobody had really expected that a bittern from the wild reed beds of Norfolk would ever feel relaxed enough to boom in a confined space, really a swampy bit of garden with low rushes, where he was always in view of the observer. Hundreds of people came to the park and literally hundreds actually watched the bittern booming, which would have been an impossible event in the wild.

Another discovery was that the bittern boomed wandering about, and not necessarily on one fixed site. It had often been claimed that a bittern boomed from a regular platform. Not so. So how could a wildlife photographer, squatting in the reed beds, ever hope to have his camera in the right place at the right time, pointing at a bittern which might boom whenever it felt like it wandering about in dense reeds? Undoubtedly the Stanstead set-up was a unique situation, unlikely to be repeated, which turned out to be one of the great triumphs of bird filming, combined with the success of caring for such wild birds in artificial circumstances. A big success for everybody all round, and I was pleased that I had had a part in it through saving the Cley bittern.

Eventually the broken-beaked bittern, which lived happily for three years, died bright-eyed and contentedly of a stroke. Lord Buxton who suddenly saw him lying flat with his head on the ground, knelt by him for an hour while he went. He really felt very strongly about that bird.

After that he brought my bittern back to Cley and we decided to release again to the wild, after his fantastic contribution to science. Before releasing this bird I marked it so as I could recognise it from a distance. It was fed for several weeks and eventually seen to catch and eat an eel. From then on I am certain it was perfectly capable of fending for itself.

New and Rare Birds

At the turn of the century, it was still possible to identify a new species of bird. The bird was usually named after its finder - Bonaparte's gull, Buffon's skua, Temminck's stint, for instance. I never had quite such good luck, but I have had my share of luck in finding three birds new, at least, to Norfolk.

During the severe winter of 1947, I was crossing the Reserve and walking along the Main Drain. Despite the fact that this drain is full of sea water, it was frozen solid. Drifting snow had formed a wall on the north side and there, sitting under the edge of this bank, were five harlequin duck, three drakes and two ducks. I could hardly believe what I saw. But there they were, these visitors in all probability from Iceland, not more than 10 feet away from me. There were large ice floes offshore that had drifted down from the north. The general opinion was that the harlequins came this far south on one of these floes. During my war service in Iceland, I had seen many of these handsome ducks but they had never before been recorded in Norfolk and I don't think they've been seen there since.

Ten years later, in 1957, again on my daily walk around the Reserve, I flushed a small wader that appeared to be, and had the call of, a common sandpiper. A little later I again saw this bird as it settled on the edge of a marshy pool. I was immediately struck by the fact that it had large, round, blackish spots on the breast and flanks, also that it showed a conspicuous white eye stripe. The legs were a dull straw colour and the proximal part of the bill was a dull orange, while the distal portion was a very dark brown. In flight, the wing pattern did not appear to differ appreciably from that of a common sandpiper. I got a tremendous thrill when I realised I was looking at a spotted sandpiper in summer plumage, an American visitor and the first recorded for Norfolk.

In the case of my other 'first', I cannot claim that I found it but only that I identified it. A bird-watcher in Blakeney asked me one evening whether it was early for a swallow to be seen in Norfolk. The date was March 6th. Of course, this is extremely early but I knew the man concerned to be knowledgeable. So the following day I went to Blakeney to try to spot this early visitor. When I found it I saw to my surprise that it had a red rump. There was no doubt this was the first record for Norfolk of the red-rumped swallow from Africa. It was later filmed by Dick Bagnall-Oakley, the well known Norfolk wildlife photographer.

It is, of course, always a great pleasure to share the first finding of a rarity with a colleague and I have had my share of good luck in this direction. With a great friend of mine, Major A. Daukes, in whose company I have spent many hours bird-watching, I found a semi-palmated sandpiper from across the Atlantic. Together, we also 'scored' the first for many years in Norfolk of the American pectoral sandpiper. This was in 1948. It has seemed strange to me that since that date they have been regular visitors. I have the feeling that they will yet be found breeding in some remote part of the British Isles.

In 1955, we found yet another rarity, the broad-billed sandpiper, and in 1961 the first red-headed bunting for Cley. This bird could have been an escape from a private aviary. In 1966, while I was close to East Bank a strange bird flew past me which proved to be a black-winged pratincole. Other exotic visitors which have flown, as it were, into my binoculars, include a long-billed dowitcher, another American wader.

I have always been attracted to birds of prey and the flight of a falcon is to me an inspiring sight. Whilst walking across the Reserve one January morning - I cannot now recall the exact date - and passing round the edge of a reed bed, I suddenly found myself face to face with a gyrfalcon, a native of Iceland and the far north. This most noble of falcons - in olden times only kings were allowed to own one - literally stood for a second and faced me with a bold stare. It is the largest and strongest of the falcons. It flew off leaving behind the remains of a water rail.

There have been a couple of times in my life when falcons have unintentionally provided me with a meal. I've twice seen a peregrine swoop and take a wild duck. On both occasions they've become scared and flown away, leaving the ducks behind. There've been many times when I've robbed herons of a big eel they've just speared from one of my dykes.

Weather Lore

A Warden needs an instinct for forecasting weather - good and bad. Along the North Norfolk Coast, we're fairly good at it. But then we and our families have lived by the weather for generations. This weather lore has been preserved in rhymes and sayings. Here are some of them: of course, it pays to watch the reading of a barometer very carefully, also!

When the rise or fall of a barometer is slow, the saying goes: 'Long foretold, long last'. When it rises or falls quickly, the message is: 'Short notice, soon past'.

If the pressure is low, we say: 'First rise after low, foretells stronger blow. When the wind shifts against the sun, (meaning that it moves anti-clockwise) trust it not for back it will run'.

With the wind in the southwest or west, you can fairly safely predict: 'Sun up. Wind up', and 'Sun down, Wind down.'

It is recognised by local farmers that during the summer months and particularly in a drought, it often looks as if it is about to rain heavily, but the clouds pass with little effect. The saying then is: 'The more the show, the less the rain.'

The next two are possibly more familiar:

'Mackerel skies and mares tails make tall ships carry small sails.'
'Mackerel sky, mackerel sky, never long wet, never long dry.'

'A red sky at night is a sailor's delight,
A red sky in the morning is a sailor's warning,
The evening red and the morning grey, are sure signs of a fine day.'

With high pressure over Scandinavia and an easterly wind developing around the time of a new moon, it is ten-to-one that the wind will more often than not be in an easterly direction until the last quarter of that moon. If it doesn't change then, it will continue to be easterly for three parts of the next moon.

'When the sun goes down behind the black, a westerly wind is on its track; but when the sun goes down as clear as a bell, it's an easterly wind as sure as hell.'

I remember one day in particular when all the signs and my own instinct told me it was going to blow like hell. And it did.

It was October 19th 1961. The barometer had been falling steadily for 72 hours with a large area of low pressure out in the North Atlantic. During the evening of the 18th, the barometer began to rise slowly. If you believe the old saying, 'first rise after low, foretells stronger blow', it seemed certain to be a wildfowler's day the following day.

Colonel Blount and Captain Buxton phoned instructions to me to meet them at the Long Drift at dawn and to bring my gun with me. I can hardly remember a more filthy morning in terms of weather or a more beautiful one for wildfowling. It was blowing a north-westerly gale and raining in torrents. At this time my own enthusiasm was waning regarding wildfowling. I was nowhere as keen as I would have been twenty years earlier. With the water running down my neck into my sea-boots, I thought it far from pleasant, although there were masses of duck about. I had few shots. My only success was one teal that was flying four behind the one I shot at! They were moving with the wind up their tails like jet fighters.

One of the finest wildfowl shots I've ever known is Major Aubrey Buxton, now Lord Buxton, who then had the shooting rights of Salthouse marshes which join the Cley marshes. On this day, he had been out since dawn on what he described to me as 'a perfect wildfowler's morning'. He had had a really good shoot and was anxious that someone else should share his enjoyment. Would I join him after breakfast?

Here was a man whose enthusiasm for wildfowling was boundless, unconcerned with being wet and cold, a first-class shot from any position and able to hide himself on a billiard table, if duck were around. He has the uncanny knack of being able to sense the exact direction a duck flight will take.

I turned down his invitation but said I would spot and pick up for him as I didn't want to shoot. I wish I'd said 'Yes'. It was a flight that wildfowlers dream of all their lives.

Three times that day he had to have a complete change of clothing and a hot bath. His day ended with a bag of ninety-six teal, 4 mallard, 10 wigeon, 1 shoveler, and 1 pintail. Some shooting, in those conditions!

I have had the good fortune of a close association with Lord Buxton for over thirty years; he is still affectionately known as 'Major Aubrey' in this part of Norfolk. During that time I have loaded for him on countless occasions. However, I would not wish to convey the impression that skill with the gun is his only attribute and I think it unfair not to mention his many activities other than in the shooting field.

He has never spared himself in playing a leading role in furthering the aims of countless movements aimed at educating the public to the importance of preserving the wildlife of countries throughout the world. He has largely done this through the medium of television; through his leadership both Anglia Television and the BBC have spread the conservation message internationally. It is a matter of pride to me that some of Anglia's world-famous *Survival* programmes have been filmed at Cley and Salthouse. One cannot make reference to this outstanding series without paying tribute to Colin Willock, *Survival's* producer and writer, whose company I have enjoyed for many happy hours on the Marshes. I have probably taught him more about marshes and wetlands than he has managed to teach me about writing!

The Menace of Vermin

Well-intentioned but perhaps misguided conservationists can unwittingly make life very difficult for a Warden. In my own case the inflexible view of a body of such people that *all* wildlife must be preserved, predatory or not, was in obvious conflict with my task and ambitions, namely to encourage the return and breeding of the rarer birds on Cley Reserve.

Nevertheless, in 1967, the protect-them-all views prevailed. The management committee of the Norfolk Naturalists Trust was persuaded to issue instructions that when black-tailed godwits appeared in the spring, all hunting and destruction of predatory vermin, even stoats, must cease. No disturbance of any kind must take place.

I had up to this time kept such vermin under strict control with one very satisfactory result: a pair of black-tailed godwits showed signs of breeding in 1965 and subsequently reared two young. Then, in 1967, when two pairs of these birds were on eggs, the ruling of the management committee was strictly enforced with the declared object of 'ensuring that these birds suffered no interference or disturbance by humans'. The result was that day after day I had to watch the parent birds fly up from their nests to hover over some villain running around their nesting sites. To me it was obvious that an animal such as a rat or a stoat was menacing the nest. No godwit has the faintest chance of defending its nest or young against a marauding bitch stoat seeking food for its own litter. But all I was allowed to do was sit and watch!

The date when the first bird began to sit was carefully recorded. After the normal passage of 24 days, the first pair of godwits hatched out their brood. Within a few hours of hatching they lost their chicks! All hope now rested on the second pair which were due to hatch three days later. Although their nest was separated from the first by some two hundred yards, the chicks suffered exactly the same fate as the first brood.

Soon after this disaster, I had the occasion to escort one of the conservationists who had been a vociferous supporter of the policy laid down by the management committee around the godwit's nesting sites. There he clearly saw the evidence that hatching had taken place in both nests. Adjacent to the site of the first nest we found the remains of a brood of young moorhen that had been mangled by a stoat. Nearby was a freshly killed adult green plover. By this time the conservationist had grown very thoughtful.

Eventually he said: 'If I hadn't seen what stoats can do with my own eyes, I wouldn't have believed it.' He fully admitted that, in ignorance of true facts, he and others like him had thought that all birds were capable of rearing their broods by themselves and that a little human help was merely interference and disturbance.

Curiously enough, black-tailed godwits, while fearless in defending their nests and young, are anything but ideal parents in the business of raising their chicks. They will happily lead them over dykes and reedbeds. If, in the process, they come up against a steep bank, the chicks are driven to scale it, often falling back exhausted into the dyke and, like as not, left to drown. Maybe survival of the fittest is at work here, but it's hard to see the benefit to the species.

Nor does it seem to dawn on the parent birds that their unfortunate practice of ceaselessly calling to their young serves as a constant attraction to local vermin. I cannot escape the feeling that a more apt name for them would be 'nitwits'.

Eventually, however, we were successful in rearing two godwit chicks and with some difficulty kept them under observation from the hatching to the flying stage. We did this despite the fact that the parent birds had dragged their chicks from their nest close to the main road, a distance of some six hundred yards, and all within 48 hours of hatching. There they were filmed by that most competent birdlife photographer, Ted Eales, then Warden of the National Trust Reserve at Blakeney Point and well known to Anglia Television viewers. Though the chicks survived, their immediate post-hatching days were more than hazardous. It was 1978 before godwits again nested at Cley with the chicks reared to the flying stage.

It is incidents such as I have just related which make me wonder whether it is always wise to follow blindly rules and regulations just because they have been formulated by a committee. Who was it once said: 'A camel is a horse that was designed by a committee?'

During the 1967 breeding season, the local ornithologists volunteered to help me form a daylight watch on the two godwits sitting on eggs and visible from the north hide. For a few days a time-table was kept without trouble after which I found many were willing to do the watching between 10 am to 12 noon and 2 pm to 4 pm. There were not many, and often none, who would stand the 5 am to 8 am watch. These unpopular times were usually filled by myself and one other ardent watcher, R.A. Richardson. One charming female helper, when asked if she would fill in the evening watch complained that it clashed with a favourite radio programme. Still, it was nice to have helpers at all.

On New Year's day, 1977, an avocet appeared on the Cley Reserve and took up residence on the north scrape. It was joined by a mate on February 5th. April 21st saw them sitting on eggs; by this time a second pair were nesting on an area known as Pat's Pool. After this came double tragedy. Both nests were robbed by rats just prior to hatching. I despatched my son Bernard to Norwich with instructions to purchase as many traps as he could get while I went to Fakenham on a similar mission.

Obviously, drastic measures had to be taken if the remaining nests were to have a chance of success. Two more pairs were sitting on eggs on the north scrape, their nesting site being surrounded by some two hundred yards of high ground. Traps were strategically set to intercept vermin while being calculated to present minimal danger to birds. Within 48 hours we accounted for three rats and a male stoat. For the remainder of the breeding season we had no more trouble with four-footed predators. The two pairs of avocets produced and reared six chicks to the flying stage.

It is always a great source of satisfaction to a Warden to have these predators well and truly under control, though I have always maintained that the man has yet to be found who can be sure that he could catch the last rat or stoat. Unfortunately, when the young of such birds are hatched it is not the end of the Warden's worries. He knows full well that there is another five weeks before the young fly, so he cannot afford to relax his vigilance.

1978 was to be my final year as Warden at Cley and I was naturally anxious for results which might bring some forty years of dedicated effort to a successful conclusion. One of my main hopes was that the black terns might stay and breed again as they had done many years earlier. This, together with the avocet and black-tailed godwit would have given me a good 'treble'. It was not to be. Nevertheless we had some remarkable successes.

An avocet unexpectedly decided that Cley was a good place to spend the winter. January 1978 brought considerable flooding. Despite this, the avocets came and 16 young were reared from six nests. April 6th saw the first pair sitting on eggs. Soon after, on looking out of my cottage window, I saw that their nesting site was covered with snow. In the face of the Arctic conditions during the incubation period, three chicks were hatched, only one of which survived.

The last nest of 1978 to hatch was on Simmond's Scrape. Approximately ten days prior to hatching, the sight was threatened with flooding during a very heavy thunderstorm which occurred in the early hours of the morning. At daybreak I found the parent birds were in a very agitated condition and had left the nest. Although it meant interference and disturbance, I knew something had to be done if the nest was to be made safe from the torrential rain and consequent flooding.

Very carefully I raised the nest a few inches by packing it from underneath and hoped for the best! The birds again returned to the nest. Unfortunately further heavy rain broke in the afternoon and this time a much bigger operation was needed to save the nest. With the help of two ornithological friends, Mr Brian Bland and Mr Steven Welch I collected a quantity of nesting material. We lifted the nest and packed the extra material underneath. This raised the whole affair some four or five inches above water level.

With considerable anxiety we waited at a safe distance to see if the parent birds would accept our interference. After what seemed ages, but was, surprisingly, only ten minutes, the parent birds again settled on the nest and eventually hatched and reared their brood. A local well-wisher who had watched the whole operation, Mr John Parrinder, from his nearby house, presented me with a bottle of Scotch as a reward.

The avocet story may be summarised as follows:

> 1979 proved to be a very successful year. Thirty young were reared from eight pairs.
> 1980: twenty nests; it was not possible to count the young reared, but it is estimated that at least fifty reached the flying stage.
> 1981: twenty-seven nests; a very wet and cold spring resulted in losing several early nests. Despite this, between fifty and sixty young were reared.

A Warden's Life

Experience has taught me that to be able to function successfully as a Warden, certain qualifications are absolutely necessary. It is nowhere near enough just to possess the ability to identify birds.

I am afraid that in the past all too frequently this one accomplishment has formed the basis on which good ornithologists have applied for the position of Warden. A Warden is not only responsible for the preservation of the birds resident on his reserve; he must also create the conditions likely to attract additional species to his area.

This requires a thorough knowledge of the habitat that will bring in and support a wide variety of species. An understanding of how to cultivate and control the vegetation is as necessary as the special skills required to keep the territory free from predators, especially during the early breeding period.

Two-legged vermin in the form of egg-collectors require extra vigilance in the breeding season. A good night's sleep for a caring Warden at this time is a rare treat. It is at this time that a Warden has to seek and welcome all the help he can get. I did receive a great deal of help during the last two years of my time as Warden. This was when the avocets returned to Cley to breed after an absence of 450 years. Unfortunately, their nesting sites were visible from the main road and public footpaths and naturally attracted a great deal of attention.

One night in 1977, a party of volunteers had stationed themselves in their car to keep watch. We'd had a tip-off that some notorious egg-collectors were in the vicinity. At about three in the morning, one of the volunteers came to my cottage and got me out of bed. He reported the arrival of a suspicious pair in a small van. I hurried to the scene with him, just in time to dissuade his rather tough companions from throwing the occupants of the van into the nearby dyke. I told them that suspicion of intent was hardly justification for such an assault. I doubt if it is realised to what extent nests are raided by egg-collectors who are able to find a lucrative market for the eggs of the rarer species.

In addition to being a guardian and, where legitimate visitors are concerned, something of a diplomat, a Warden must also be a handyman. There are many prospective Wardens who have mastered the art of using a pair of field-glasses but who have no idea how to handle a spade efficiently.

The joys and delights of late spring and summer bird-watching enjoyed by all on the reserve are only made possible by the dedicated attention given to the reserve by the Wardens during the bleak and often grim winter months. It is at this time that the Warden has to set about the tasks of repairing the devastation resulting from flooding, ice, snow, etc. Hides are frequently blown down and bridges and footpaths leading to them destroyed. Though I love the outdoors, I am prepared to state that this is not the most enjoyable part of a Warden's life!

Earlier, I referred to the importance of vegetation and habitat control. A somewhat special aspect of this concerns the advisability or otherwise of allowing cattle on the reserve to graze under proper supervision. Where ducks and waders are concerned, I have always maintained and believed grazing to be wholly beneficial. If no other good comes of it, it keeps the vegetation under control. Without this, the area would become a paradise for vermin, making control of the predators much more difficult. Grazing animals leave behind a deposit of rich fertiliser on the ground, which in turn encourages the production of insects so necessary to the feeding of some species. When, in my childhood days, some fifty thousand sheep were grazed on the saltings between Cley and the Wash, at least as many golden plover were to be found feeding there during the winter months. The sheep went and with them the golden plover. Likewise the grey geese which also used to winter there in great numbers though in their case there were probably other causes as well. Cattle can, of course, constitute a danger to ground-nesting birds but only if the beasts are unduly disturbed by some unusual event or perhaps by an invasion of flies. I have seen a redshank sitting on its nest pick at the snout of an intruding cow to encourage it to graze elsewhere!

Reeds, so important to such species as bitterns, bearded tits, bunting, and warblers, are they subject of frequent debate. Should they be cut or left uncut? It has been argued that, in some years, the lack of breeding bitterns is due to excessive reed-cutting. This was put forward by many as the main reason for the absence of bitterns in 1970. My own belief (and this was later backed up by official opinion), is that the barren period resulted from the devastation of the bittern in the terrible winter of 1963, when at least 95 per cent of the bitterns in the country were wiped out. I do not think a bittern breeds under three years old, and only then if it is in a strong and healthy condition. There weren't many survivors who met these requirements in 1970.

Reed-cutting continued at Cley despite the arguments and the booming of the bittern was heard once again in 1971. Somewhat reluctantly, the management of the Reserve agreed to stop cutting reeds for a trial period. It looked as though the anti-cutting lobby had won the day. Before long, though, it became clear that lack of cutting resulted in a marked deterioration of the reed-beds, so the embargo was lifted. Reed-cutting was resumed and once again the bearded tits were seen flocking around the reed-cutters and enjoying the feed that was released in the process. The reed-beds are now flourishing and the bitterns continue to increase. At least two and possibly three nests were successful in 1978. The birds have bred every year since. Once again, it illustrates the point that a reserve is a limited area whose habitat must be managed if it is to produce the best results for its wild inhabitants.

I have tried to explain some of the problems which a Warden on a reserve has to contend with. I've described the long hours of patient work he is called upon to put in if he is to do his job properly. But life for a Warden is very far from being all toil and worry. Quite often there comes the chance to enjoy a unique ornithological experience. That's

1. C. D. Borrer and Frank Izod Richards

2. The old 'Britannia'

3. A case from the Richards collection

4. H. N. Pashley in 1921, aged 77, with his grandchildren

5. E. C. Arnold

6. Ted Ramm

7. Dr. Sidney Long

£5100 FOR BIRD SANCTUARY.

PURCHASE OF CLEY MARSHES.

An interesting announcement was made at the conclusion of the sale at the Royal Hotel, Norwich, on Saturday afternoon of the wild fowling marshes on the Norfolk coast, a portion of the Cley Hall estate, now sold by Messrs. John D. Wood & Co., of London, by instructions from the executors of the late Mr. A. W. Cozens-Hardy. The first lot, that of 407 acres, was sold for £5100 to Dr. S. Long, who told our representative at the conclusion of the sale that he was acting on behalf of a group of ornithologists who had in mind the project of a bird sanctuary there. Dr. Long also bought for £60 a freehold building site adjoining and containing 1r. 8p.

Other lots disposed of were a 27 acre marsh situate in Cley and Salthouse to Mr. Ratcliffe for £210; a freehold building site 1r. 24p. to Mr. Stangroom for £60, and another building site, also freehold and containing 1r. 23p., to Mr. Loines for £50.

Messrs. Cozens-Hardy & Jewson were the solicitors acting.

9. The Eastern Daily Press of March 8th 1926 reported the purchase of the Marshes by Dr. Long. [Photo: Eastern Daily Press]

CLEY-NEXT-THE-SEA,
NORFOLK,

Four miles from Holt Town and Station, 1 mile from Blakeney, 10 miles from Wells, and 12 miles from Cromer.

UNIQUE

Wild Fowling Marshes

ON THE NORFOLK COAST,

being a portion of the

CLEY HALL ESTATE,

and comprising a total area of about

435 ACRES

running down to and including the foreshore, forming

A WILD FOWL DAY-FEEDING GROUND,

including

MARSHES, REED-BEDS, SALTINGS, SOME ARABLE LAND AND BUILDING SITES,

WHICH

are, unless previously disposed of by private contract, instructed by the Executors of Arthur Wrigley Cozens-Hardy, deceased, to offer by Auction.

Messrs. **JOHN D. WOOD & CO.,**
6 Mount Street, LONDON, W.1.,

At the ROYAL HOTEL, Norwich,
On Saturday, March 6th, 1926,
At 2.0 p.m.

Solicitors:
Messrs. COZENS-HARDY & JEWSON, Norwich.

Land Agents:
Messrs. FRANCIS HORNOR & SON, Norwich.

Auctioneers' Offices: 6 Mount Street, LONDON, W.1.

8. Notice of the sale by auction of Cley Marshes

10. Robert Bishop, the first Watcher at Cley

11. Billy Bishop with Bittern chick

12. Major Aubrey Buxton with Billy Bishop the morning after the flight of October 20th 1961

13. A seal cull: Billy Bishop with Ted Eales, Warden of Blakeney Point

14. Lord and Lady Alanbrooke and Dick Bagnall-Oakeley preparing for a filming session

15. The 1953 Flood: Cley village

16. The 1953 Flood: The Reserve

17. Coypu hunt, 1971. Over 6000 of these 20 lb rodents were taken on the Reserve between 1947 and 1978

18. Billy and Bernard Bishop at work on the Main Drain

19. The opening of the Dick Bagnall-Oakeley Memorial Centre: Bernard Bishop with Jane-Anne Walton (daughter of Dick Bagnall-Oakeley) and the broadcaster Robert Dougall
[Photo: Eastern Daily Press]

20. The 1996 Flood: The new hides

21. The 1996 Flood: At Old Woman's Lane

22. The clear-up: Bernard Bishop

23. NWT staff from Hickling salvaging sections of boardwalk at the Coast Road

24. HRH The Prince of Wales with Bernard Bishop during his official visit on March 28th 1996
[Photo: Eastern Daily Press]

one of the things that makes the jobs so well worthwhile. Equally rewarding is the chance to meet great naturalists.

Quite early in my employment as Warden at Cley, I was offered, together with the Warden of Hickling, Ted Piggin, the opportunity of visiting reserves in Holland as the guests of Mr J.C. Cadbury, a well-known and very knowledgeable ornithologist. It proved to be a memorable treat. We saw many species which at that time were rarities in the United Kingdom. We saw spoonbills, ruffs and reeves and black-tailed godwits in great numbers, often on their nesting sites.

During my long spell as Warden at Cley, my holidays were used to learn more of the habitat of birds. Having spent seventeen months around the Icelandic coast during the war years, where my interest in birds helped to keep me sane, I promised myself that if ever it became possible, I would like to return to Iceland and study the birdlife in peacetime, and this happened when Mr and Mrs Bernard Simmonds invited me to join them on a tour of Iceland. It is a bird-lover's paradise, an island with a crystal-clear atmosphere and spectacular scenery with its volcanoes and glaciers.

One of my main ambitions was to see and possibly film the grey phalarope in breeding plumage, Iceland being the only place in Europe where this species breeds. Both the grey and red-necked phalaropes visit Cley fairly regularly, chiefly in the autumn. So I had yet to see one in breeding plumage. Red-necked phalaropes are almost as common in Iceland as the redshank is in the United Kingdom. But only in one small area on the south coast of Iceland did we find the grey phalarope.

Six of the fourteen days were spent at Myvatn, the so-called 'Lake of Flies'. This is most certainly the Mecca for all ornithologists keen on water birds. In summer there are vast hatches of small black flies and midges to provide food for nesting birds and their young. Fast-running streams flow out of the lake itself. Harlequin ducks abound; so do mergansers and their young. On the lake are many thousands of duck and I was struck with the thought that there was never need to worry about a world shortage of duck while such places as Myvatn exist. There were throngs of mallard, wigeon, eiders, tufted, Barrow's goldeneye, scaup, long-tailed duck, gadwall and mergansers, and around them snow buntings and wheatears and half-a- dozen pairs of great northern divers. I found only one pair of gyr falcons. This bird, the national emblem of Iceland, is strictly under guard at all times. Not many years ago, a visiting ornithologist stole some gyr eyasses from the eyrie and got away with it. Iceland has never forgotten this.

Having enjoyed our trip to Iceland, these same two generous people decided that on a future occasion we should visit that wonderful reserve in southern Spain, the Coto Donana. We would follow the same route through Spain that had been taken earlier by those great photographers and ornithologists, Roger Tory Peterson, Guy Mountford, Lord Alanbrooke, Eric Hosking, James Ferguson-Lees, James Fisher, E.R. (John) Parrinder, Jerry Jamieson and George Shannon. A a result of these enthusiasts' previous tour, Spain had been persuaded, with the help of the World Wildlife Fund, to make the Coto a national park.

In 1973, we set out from the Algarve in Portugal by Range Rover for the Coto Donana. I had been Warden at Cley by this time for thirty-seven years, and to see a new bird had become a rare event. But on this trip I clocked up twenty-five species new to me. The first three hours were the most eventful I have ever spent, seeing at least fifty black kites, hundreds of cattle egrets, black-winged stilts, black vultures, rollers, spoonbills, little egrets, European bee-eaters, fan-tail warblers, short-toed larks and a pair of Spanish imperial eagles, the rarest of European eagles. Most of the terns were either gull-billed or whiskered. The kestrels were lesser kestrels and the starlings were all spotless starlings.

As to meeting great naturalists I have had more than my share of fortune here, too. Outstanding among these will always be Arthur Patterson of Great Yarmouth. He used to visit my father whenever he came to our area. I was a schoolboy at the time. I remember him presenting my father with autographed copies of his famous books, among them *On the Broads*, a book that I treasure and have never tired of reading. I regret that I did not keep some of his many articles that were regularly published in the *Eastern Daily Press*. As a schoolboy, I looked upon Arthur Patterson as a hero and remember the great thrill I got when he asked to see my egg collection. Nowadays, of course, schoolboys know better than to collect birds' eggs and, anyway, it's against the law. In my youth, things were different - I had a good collection of local birds' eggs and gave them to the school when I left at the age of fourteen. One of the prizes of my collection was a wryneck's egg (I shudder to think of it now) that I had taken from the nest in the Butts Plantation at Blakeney, around 1925. Today, I realise that this could well have been the last time a wryneck nested in this area.

I was also fortunate to have been able to have spent a good deal of time with the late Jim Vincent of Hickling who was perhaps the best man I ever knew at finding nests. One fine afternoon, we sat together on Walsey Hills overlooking Cley and Salthouse marshes. After an hour's waiting, Jim got up and said: 'Now we will look at a redshank's, green plover's, ringed plover's and a garganey's nest.' He then led me to all four nests which he had spotted during our vigil. He would stand in an area where he had seen a bird disappear, look around and say: 'If I were a bird, I would put my nest there', pointing to a spot. Sure enough that was just where the nest usually was. Lessons such as he gave I have never forgotten.

There was a time when I was doubtful whether a small wader was a Temminck's or a little stint, and Jim gave me a valuable tip to prove its identity. He told me to flush the bird and explained what it would do, saying that if it was a Temminck's it would fly up fairly high and twist and turn in the air like a butterfly before it settled again; it would also show its white outer tail feathers and call loudly. On the other hand, if it was a little stint, its call would be much weaker. It would show no outer white tail feathers and it would fly away in level flight. Any knowledge I have built up since has been founded on the principles taught me by such mentors.

I have been most fortunate in having met and known intimately great nature-loving sportsmen from all walks of life. The love of the outdoors and all the sports that are associated with it is something which seems to attract the sort of people who, irrespective of social standing, are invariably grand in every sense of the word, men like Sir Henry Birkin, Sir Henry Upcher, Lord Leicester and Colin McLean. These come readily to my mind along with many others. It was largely due to their foresight and generosity that the Cley Reserve is what it is today. The numbers of duck they shot were small indeed compared with the numbers given feeding and resting grounds by their acts of conservation.

I have had the pleasure of accompanying members of the Royal Family, including Prince Philip and Prince Charles. Prince Philip especially has a great love of wildfowling and of wildfowl. I well remember the first time he came to Salthouse marshes, next door to the Reserve and not part of it, as the guest of Lord Buxton, together with Lord Leicester and Colonel R. Buxton. It was on October 11th 1956, and great preparations had been made to ensure a successful occasion. I had sunk a large barrel into the marsh that had previously contained rum, for HRH to use as a hide. Around this was a mass of sea aster. I won't report what he said about the smell of rum, but as he settled in his hide, he remarked that he had shot duck in many places but this was the first time he had ever done so from the middle of an herbaceous border.

When you go out to shoot duck at evening flight, you hope for a strong wind, preferably from the sea. The rough water forces the duck to seek the shelter of the marshes and land. As luck would have it, on this particular night there was a dead calm. A true wildfowler enjoys it no matter the number of duck. Prince Philip had a wonderful time and didn't hesitate to say so, even though the pick-up after the flight was pretty slender.

During migration periods, HRH regularly visited Cley Reserve with his field glasses. He is just as keen to watch waders as he is to shoot duck. He was so impressed by our efforts to create the sort of habitat that would lure back some of the breeding waders Norfolk had lost, that he arranged for myself and Peter Newland, who dug out the Cley scrapes, to take his machines over to the royal estate at Wolferton. There we made a similar set of shallow pools. I certainly believe that the potential is as good there. So if the avocets and black-tailed godwits continue to increase in Norfolk, as in the past few years, they will most certainly spread to the west and to the royal estate.

One of the eminent wildlife photographers it has been my pleasure to meet was the late Lord Alanbrooke, the famous Field Marshall of the Second World War. I have never met a more patient man. I used to escort him to his hide overlooking an area where he hoped some waders would come to feed. He was quite content to sit there with his camera for eight to ten hours. He took quite a lot of good film and gave me some footage which I still have in my possession.

There are few, if any, ornithologists of my generation who have not heard of Professor Maury Meiklejohn. He was one of the finest and most humorous ornithologists of his day. Anyone who spent any time with him could not help learning something. He wrote many natural history articles for various journals and was a regular visitor to Cley Reserve. To Maury, everyone was 'such a nice person'. 'M.F.M.M.' became a legend in his lifetime. He died in Glasgow at the early age of sixty-one. Maury was widely known for his wit and his writing of humorous stories, many of which I have in my possession. He was one of the most knowledgeable ornithologists of his day. Despite the fact that he never carried a gun, the last of the Gentlemen Gunners were his friends.

He served for many years on the British Rarities Committee, who were nicknamed 'The Ten Rare Men'. Many of his friends at Cley will remember him as a rather stout person, walking briskly along the foreshore clad in an assortment of pullovers, corduroy trousers and heavy boots, more often than not hatless. Either that, or sitting in the corner of the local sipping his pint of mild beer and smoking a pipe.

Maury enlisted in the South African Army in 1941 and often joked that the only time he ever fired a shot in anger was at a hyena that had kept him awake at night. He was the creator of the bird called the 'Hoodwink' which was never identified as it always flew off, sat in a bad light, or was just out of range of the best binoculars.

He wrote many amusing verses regarding bird watchers - the classic being 'Are You A Bird Watcher?', in which he teases the car-borne rarity hunter. It is illustrated with a motorist looking from a fast-moving car.

'I met a rufous turtle-dove at Westbury-on-Trym,
I took my little notebook and I sat and studied him.
I examined all his feathers with 7-35's,
Then I drove on to see a limpkin that was stranded at St. Ives.
Next day I found an albatross at Ashby-de-la-Zouche:
A crowd arrived from Leicester in a motorised barouche.
They got there twenty minutes late, I told them what they'd missed
I ticked off a BB albatross - 300th on my list.

*With my foot hard on the pedal I made a record time
To notch a collared flycatcher at Ashton-under-Lyne.'*

*'I had seen the brown already but this was new to me,
But a garbage man had shot it, and had it for his tea.
So then I went to Aldershot to find some azure tits:
My notes compelled the 'Ten Rare Men' to have ten azure fits.
But there are rare birds yet to see before the other folks,
Before I go to Paradise by way of Perry Oaks.'*

*'Hoorah! Hoorah! My British List now stands at three-o-five -
I've seen as many rarities as anyone alive.
I don't know where they live or nest or what their habits are,
For - fancy this - I've seen them without getting from my car.'*

*'From end to end of Britain I drive without a rest,
Which means, of course you realise, that I've never found a nest.
But once I saw a robin and heard its tuneful call,
Though I've never seen a blackbird or a hedge sparrow at all.'*

During a lifetime spent wholly, with the exception of the war years, close to nature in my part of Norfolk, I have experienced a good deal out of the ordinary. The rewards of such a life are certainly more to the spirit than to the pocket. That great literary figure, Hilaire Belloc, left us his epitaph: 'In this world, nothing is worth the toil of winning save laughter and the love of friends.'

On this basis, I reckon I am a millionaire. It has been my good fortune to meet and work with many famous as well as ordinary folk whom I am proud to include among the host of friends who have given me great happiness. As for laughter, we have all shared that on many occasions!

Some Tips on Identification

To end my account of my life as Warden of Cley Marshes, I will give a complete list of all the species, rare and common, that have been recorded there. Some of the 'firsts' I have been lucky enough to spot and identify myself. I am often asked by visitors how to go about identifying birds that mystify them at first sight. Very well, then. Here is my way of tackling that often bewildering task.

Far too often the inexperienced bird-watcher relies on two or three criteria in an attempt to identify a bird. Usually, these are: colouration, length and shape of bill, length and colour of leg, etc. Having established these, there often still remains an uncertainty as to positive identification. When, as frequently happens, such doubts are expressed to me, I invariably ask three questions. First: 'What size was it?' Second: 'Exactly where was it seen?' Lastly: 'What was it doing?' From the answer to these questions I can usually find out to which family it belongs.

Establishment of such characteristics are vital to accurate identification. Some species will seek to hide in thick cover; others deliberately choose not to do so and will perch on top of cover rather than in it. Some will run on open ground; others will walk or hop. For instance, all the plover family will give a short run followed by an abrupt stop. The experienced ornithologist will invariably look for such identification criteria. You will note that I have not dealt with colouration. This is because plumage changes can occur with the seasons more so than habit and habitat.

After watching coastal birds for fifty years, one gets to know how they fly and feed. I have read on several occasions that the flight of a ruff or reeve is like that of a redshank. I don't agree and have often changed a bird-watcher's notes to read: 'Flight *un*like redshank'. A ruff has a much lazier flight and will often sideslip.

In the autumn, young dunlin are often mistaken at first glance for little stints. But, on closer observation, one sees that little stints feed much quicker and usually on the drier areas of mud. I have always considered that the sanderling feeds half as fast again as the dunlin and the little stint twice as fast.

To identify waders it is a big advantage to learn recognition of the common ones really well and then you can say to yourself: 'I don't know what it is, but I do know what it *isn't*.' There are many waders of approximately the same size as dunlin and redshank. Therefore, to learn these two really well puts one at an advantage.

I have always advised beginners, old or young, to learn the call notes so that they can use ears as well as eyes. This has stood me in good stead during my years as Warden.

To learn just one habit of any particular bird really well also has its advantages: for instance, when identifying a jack snipe from a common snipe. When flushed, the common snipe normally rises well in front and will call before flying well away from you. The jack snipe rises from almost under your feet. If it calls, it is a very weak call. It can be guaranteed to settle again, if the ground is suitable, within 200 yards.

I am often asked how to identify a green from a wood sandpiper. These birds migrate to Cley at the same time of the year and are about the same size. Unless one is using a hide, the green sandpiper will not allow you to approach within 50 yards. The wood sandpiper is less sensitive and will often allow a much closer approach, say, to within 30 yards. The green sandpiper has always reminded me of an oversized house martin with its prominent white rump and black upper parts. I have never known why we in Britain have fallen in step with the Americans in naming some of our waders, an example being Bonaparte's sandpiper. The Americans changed it to the white-rumped

SOME TIPS ON IDENTIFICATION

sandpiper. Maybe it is because they have only one sandpiper with a white rump where we have others.

Many people ask me how to tell the difference between a reed warbler and a sedge warbler. The issue hinges round which one has the eye stripe. My answer is: 'Stripe starts with the letter "S", so does "sedge".' It couldn't be simpler to remember.

The three main terns of our Norfolk coast sometimes cause problems of identification, though of course they're very easy to tell apart, at least by the experienced ornithologist. The little tern is identified by its much smaller size. The largest of the three, the sandwich tern, is much whiter than its two cousins. The third, the common tern, is much greyer and halfway in size between the other two. Of course, we occasionally get Arctics, too. They can be confused with common terns. If you see them clearly enough, you'll spot that the bill is plain red without a black tip. The outer tail coverts are longer, too.

As mentioned previously, the flight of the ruff and reeve differs from that of the redshank. The ruff (as you'll know, the females are called reeves) has the habit of standing erect when sensing danger, unlike any other wader, with the exception of the American pectoral sandpiper which is a much smaller bird and a rare visitor.

Harriers are often confused. The marsh harrier quarters its feeding area more thoroughly than its relatives and usually from a slightly greater height. Also the hen harrier and Montagu harrier fly faster as well as lower.

Identification of the wild swans can be simple if one remembers that it is the larger swan, the whooper, that has the larger amount of yellow on the bill, extending beyond the nostril, whereas the yellow on the bill of the Bewick's swan stops at the nostril. When in flight the mute swan's wings vibrate with a sound like the rattling of tin cans.

If all the foregoing sounds laborious, you must remember that perfection in any craft is never achieved without effort, but the effort can be very rewarding. These are just a few straightforward tips to be going on with. Now here is the complete list of what has already been seen at Cley. Who knows? - you may be able to add to it.

Extracts from the Warden's Diary 1937 - 1981
Billy Bishop

CLEY MARSH AND ITS BIRDS

1937

To meet the cost of running the Reserve during its earlier days, the grazing rights were let to local farmers, the sporting rights to local wildfowlers. Reeds were to be cut and sold for thatching. The cutting of reed took place during the first three months of the year. The men were paid two pence per bunch to cut and carry the reed to places where it could be picked up by lorry or cart. Carriers were paid one shilling per hour for carting with horse and cart to the main road.

The total of wild fowl shot over the Reserve during 1937 was 265 ducks and 35 snipe. A pair of shorteared owls nested on the Reserve to the east of Taylor's hill during May of that year and reared six young.

1938

On January 11th, at a time of spring tides, a severe north-west gale occurred, the wind reaching 80 - 90 miles per hour. It blew for 36 hours and on the afternoon of the 12th, with the wind still at gale force and with the big tides, the heavy seas came sweeping over the top of the beach two hours before the time of high water. Cley Reserve was flooded to the depth of 7 - 8 feet. The East Bank was broken in three places. Despite this, the water level was back to normal within fourteen days, and 6,000 bunches of reed were still harvested during February and March.

During June, the keeper of Salthouse marshes reported a pair of dunlin with young. On June 11th, Dr Long, the founder of the Norfolk Naturalists' Trust, Miss Gay, his secretary and myself, visited the area. In the words of Dr Long: 'The parent birds flew around us very agitated, the flight being like that of a snipe. They uttered a whirring trill when flying, quite unlike the ordinary call of a dunlin. We had little doubt that the young were crouching in the grass nearby.' Mr W. Holman had seen one young on June 5th and a Mr Kenrick one the following day. A young dunlin, almost fully fledged was later found dead by Mr Holman. It had been trodden on by a horse and was taken by Dr Long to Castle Museum, Norwich.

Redbacked shrike nested this year in what is now the Norfolk Naturalists' Trust car park but once was known as the Marl Pit. Kingfishers nested in the bank of the Main Drain at Salthouse.

During the early hours of June 30th, a stoat killed sixteen adult common terns on their nests on Arnold's Marsh. Mr Holman reported a second brood of dunlin on Salthouse marshes on July 11th but this brood was never confirmed. One hundred and ninety-five duck and forty-two snipe were shot on Cley Marsh during this season.

1939

Bitterns nested on Salthouse for the first time for many years and two bitterns' nests were found in reeds opposite the Watcher's Cottage.

There were 119 sandwich terns' nests with eggs on May 8th. Mr Holman and myself made the final count on June 2nd and found 1,042 nests with eggs and chicks.

There were three stone curlews' nests within three miles of Cley.

The opening date of the season for duck shooting was put back from August 1st to August 12th. (Note: Since 1954, it has been September 1st.)

1939 - 45

Records for Cley for the next six years are incomplete, as I was away from the Reserve on war service.

A major flood occurred during April 1943, which caused the sandwich terns to move from Arnold's Marsh and settle to breed in the middle of a mine field on Cley Beach. Needless to say, they were not molested by humans. But, after two years, they again moved for no apparent reason to the west. With the exception of the odd pair, they have not returned to breed up to the present date (1982) in any numbers.

The Cley Reserve was taken over by the military in early 1940 and the two brick bridges that spanned the Main Drain were blown up. Large concrete pill-boxes were placed on top and at each side of the East Bank and a defensive wall of tubular scaffolding was erected from Weybourne to the Cley Channel to repel possible landings by German tanks.

Reed was sold during the war years for the manufacture of paper.

An army camp was built on the Eye field (see historical notes, Appendix A) during the early part of the war with heavy gun sites and other sea defences along the north boundary.

1946

The army camp on the Eye field was now being used for prisoners of war, mostly Italian. Some of the prisoners were employed by the Norfolk Naturalists Trust to work on the Reserve, reed cutting, etc. That year over 8,000 bunches were cut.

On June 12th six bitterns were seen sunning themselves along the edge of the reed bed and I was shown a brood of quail by Mr W. Brett on June 15th on Cley Hall Farm. Redbacked shrike were still nesting at the south end of the East Bank. 1946 was a curlew sandpiper year. It was estimated that over 250 of these birds were present in mid-September.

Eleven bitterns were seen flying around the Reserve at dusk on September 16th. Bearded tits were found at Cley by Major Aubrey Buxton, on November 9th.

1947

Very heavy snow fell during the first two months of the year and it was estimated that 95 per cent of the moorhens on the reserve perished with the cold. The bittern population was reduced and survivors were artificially fed.

Stone curlew again nested on Cley Hall Farm.

At least a hundred pairs of mallard nested on the reserve and five pairs of garganey. Six pairs of little terns nested on the shingle ridge north of Arnold's Marsh.

1948

It was estimated that eighteen to twenty pairs of garganey were present on Cley on March 21st and between twenty and twenty-five pairs on March 23rd. But only nine pairs stayed to breed.

The Round Pond was excavated by dragline during the later part of June.

Redbacked shrike were again breeding on two areas around the reserve.

Fulmars had increased and were breeding on Weybourne cliffs. Ledges were made in the cliffs by Capt. R. Bagnall-Oakeley and pupils from Gresham's School, Holt, in an effort to encourage these birds to increase. (Bagnall-Oakeley was a master at Gresham's and a passionate ornithologist. He and his film appeared many times on the BBC in East Anglia.)

A survey of nests of several species was undertaken by Capt. Bagnall-Oakeley and myself on June 23rd. This established that three pairs of stone curlew, fourteen pairs of redbacked shrike and twenty-five pairs of yellow wagtail were breeding either on the Reserve or within one mile of it.

Gadwall were proved to be breeding on the Reserve for the first time in my recollection.

Eighty young shellduck with one pair of parent birds were recorded on July 2nd.

Bearded tits were found to be breeding by Major Daukes, Mrs Meiklejohn and myself.

A pectoral sandpiper was found by Major Daukes at Salthouse. This bird eventually found its way into Mr Borrer's private collection of stuffed birds.

1949

A major flood occurred on March 1st, the wind veering north-west and reaching gale force during the early hours. Heavy seas swept over the shingle ridge from Blakeney Point to Weybourne, flooding the Cley Reserve to the depth of 6 - 7 feet and Salthouse marshes to 12 - 14 feet. The villages of Cley, Salthouse, Morston and Blakeney were flooded. The East Bank was broken in five places and a breach was made in the beach near Taylor's Hill, allowing the tide to ebb and flow, temporarily making the Reserve tidal. The breach was sealed with the help of a bulldozer five weeks later.

Bitterns and bearded tits took refuge in the woods of Cley Hall Farms. By March 3rd the floodwater had receded by 2 feet on both Cley and Salthouse.

Water level on Cley was back to normal by the 9th, despite the tide flowing in and out through the breach at high water. But the spring tides from the 12th to the 18th brought a new rise of water over the Reserve from 6 inches to 4 feet and the breach in the beach widened to

50 yards and 8 feet deep at high water. This gap slowly filled up during the following neap tides and was eventually closed by bulldozers.

Four pairs of stone curlews nested on Kelling Heath and another pair on Cley Hall Farm.

Redbacked shrike bred in what is now the Norfolk Naturalists car park.

A water rail with brood was seen on Cley on July 5th.

The first Canada goose arrived at Cley on November 27th and a white-tailed sea eagle was observed along the north boundary at the end of the month.

1950

A sea eagle was present on and around the Reserve from January 16th to 20th.

A note on March 21st records that at least twenty pairs of woodlark were nesting around Salthouse Heath. At the time of writing (1982) these birds are no longer to be seen there.

Five bittern nests were established on May 20th and twenty pairs of redbacked shrike found within 3 miles of Cley.

Fifty-eight pairs of house martins nested on the Watcher's Cottage.

An effort to introduce sedge to grow on Cley was made on September 26th but this failed owing to the saline conditions.

1951

Redbacked shrike nested again in the Marl Pit.

An invasion of wood sandpiper on August 8th. At least sixty were in evidence on Cley.

In the course of the first three days in October a very large movement of birds was observed at Cley.

That first-class ornithologist, my friend Major Daukes, wrote a detailed account of this exceptional landfall of birds which I now quote in full. It gives an excellent and accurate picture of this phenomenon. Major Daukes writes:

> The last few days of September consisted mostly of fair weather with easterly winds, due to the existence of an anticyclone over Norway.

During the night of September 30th/October 1st, a steady easterly wind prevailed, accompanied by considerable low cloud. These conditions continued during the day of October 1st but, with the exception of a few chaffinches and redstarts, nothing of particular interest occurred during that morning. About 1 pm, however, the ruins of the camp at the end of the Beach Road at Cley and the bushes and buildings between the road and the Observatory were suddenly swarming with robins. We estimated that there were at least 200 in the Camp buildings alone, in addition to vastly larger numbers in the grass, the bushes and buildings in the neighbourhood of the Observatory. By evening, 102 robins had been ringed by the Warden and his assistants.

In the course of the afternoon many robins were observed coming in from the sea in a very exhausted condition and could have been picked up by hand. One bird was seen to come in very low over the water and, unable to gain height, collided with a low ridge of shingle just above the tide mark.

Between 3 pm and 5 pm on the same day, the bushes suddenly became alive with goldcrests and song thrushes, although these were not actually seen to come in from the sea.

On October 2nd, after a night of continued medium to strong easterly winds and cloud, I went along the beach towards Blakeney Point. In the bushes from the Hood to the Long Hills were masses of birds including a very large number of robins, song thrushes, goldcrests (among which one firecrest was observed), a fair number of redwings, fieldfares, bramblings, chaffinches, redstarts, willow wrens and/or chiffchaffs, blackcaps (male and female), one ring ousel (cock) and five bluethroats, one of which was in practically full spring plumage with blue breast and red spots.

The following day, October 3rd, was fine and cloudless, with a steady east wind, after a night of similar conditions. The Hood, the Long Hills and the Britannia Ridge produced a great many robins and goldcrests, but fewer than on the previous days. There were much larger numbers than previously of song thrushes, redwings, fieldfares with a fair number of blackbirds, twenty to thirty ring ousels, some bramblings, chaffinches, blackcaps, redstarts, a few willow wrens and/or chiffchaffs, one pied flycatcher, one spotted flycatcher, one merlin and two bluethroats (immature). The small plantation on the Point, near the Laboratory, was flushed out and produced (simultaneously) twenty to twenty-five goldcrests, eight ring ousels, a few willow wrens or chiffchaffs and one short-eared owl.

By the following day, October 4th, with similar weather conditions prevailing, most of the birds appeared to have passed on.

There are, of course, on record many cases of migration on a large or larger scale and productive of more and much greater rarities, but two points of interest emerge in this instance.

1) It was only when the easterly winds were accompanied by low cloud and mist that very large numbers of many species of birds were observed.

2) That robins were seen coming in from the sea during the middle of the day, while, judging from the time at which they appeared, everything pointed to the song thrushes and goldcrests having done so as well, although this was not actually observed

1952

A redrumped swallow was filmed by R.P. Bagnall-Oakeley on June 7th; he also filmed a little egret on Cley on May 8th.

A broad-billed sandpiper was identified at Cley, Norfolk on June 5th. The bird was first seen among a small flock of dunlin, when one bird was observed to be without a black belly. The birds were stalked until, at a range of 20 yards, every detail could be seen clearly.

The sandpiper was apparently still a bird in winter plumage, the back and wings being ashy-brown in colour with reeve-like markings. The chin was greyish white, as were the underparts. The breast was streaked, the streaks ending rather abruptly. It was smaller than the dunlin and stood lower. The bill and legs appeared brownish black. By far the most conspicuous features of the bird, however, were the heavily striped appearance of the head and the fact that the bill, which was slightly decurved, appeared to have a most definite downward bend - almost a hook - towards the end. The bill did not give any particular impression of breadth as the bird's name suggests.

The head, which was somewhat reminiscent of that of the American pectoral sandpiper, was entirely unmistakable and consisted of a dark crown, bordered with pale margins, which were separated from the whitish supercilliary stripes by a narrow dark line, giving a remarkably striped appearance. The wing pattern in flight did not appear to be noticeably different from that of the dunlins, although the difference in size was obvious. No song was heard, unfortunately.

1952 proved to be a year of rarities: in addition to the broad-billed sandpiper, a night heron and a little bittern were observed.

1953

Another major flood occurred at the end of January with a north-west gale on the 31st, the wind reaching 120 miles per hour. Cley village and Salthouse were inundated and water flowed up the Glaven valley for 3 miles. All low-lying house were flooded, some up to 8 feet. The flood water came up to the back door of the Watcher's Cottage. The Reserve was flooded to a depth of 10 - 12 feet. All banks between Salthouse and Morston were breached in may places and there were five new breaches in the East Bank. The shingle ridge was moved back at least 50 yards. One hundred and sixty house in Cley and Newgate, fifty in Salthouse, and three in Glandford and Wiveton were flooded.

A former lifeboat that had been moored at the north end of Blakeney Harbour broke from her moorings and came to rest 400 yards to the south of Wiveton Stone Bridge, having drifted across the Wiveton marshes and over the main Cley to Blakeney road.

The water level fluctuated wildly with the tide for several days and was not back to normal until February 21st. Nevertheless, bitterns returned to the Reserve by the end of February and later bred successfully. Bearded tits did not breed during 1953 but returned to the Reserve on October 19th.

1954

When walking across the Reserve on January 1st, I came face to face with an Icelandic falcon (gyr) feeding on the remains of a water rail it had evidently killed. For a split second I thought it would attack me but it finally flew off towards Blakeney Harbour.

Bearded tits did not breed during 1954 and again appeared in the autumn.

Woodpigeons in large numbers were once more observed coming in over the beach from a north-east direction during the early hours. Where do they come from? There is always a lot of controversy as to whether the migration is from the north of England or from Northern

Europe or Scandinavia. Yet there are said to be comparatively few woodpigeons there: certainly nothing like the flocks we get here.

1955

At least ten bitterns were resident at Cley and four were booming on May 8th. In October, a case brought to prevent local wildfowlers shooting on the East Bank was settled in favour of the Norfolk Naturalists Trust.

1956

The first collared doves were found breeding at Overstrand on July 5th.

1957

On June 5th I was making my daily round of the marshes at Cley when I saw on the wing what appeared to be a common sandpiper. A little later I again saw the bird, which had by then settled on the edge of a marshy pool. I was immediately struck by the fact that it had large round, blackish spots on the breast and flanks: also that it had a conspicuous white eye stripe. The legs were dull straw-coloured and the proximal part of the bill was dull orange, while the distal portion was very dark brown. The wing pattern in flight did not appear to differ appreciably from that of a common sandpiper.

There was no doubt that the bird was a spotted sandpiper in summer plumage. It flew in a manner similar to a common sandpiper. Its note was not unlike that of a common sandpiper but from time to time it made a double note 'peet-weet'.

Subsequently I had it under observation for a considerable period at distances of less than 10 yards. It was later seen by Mrs R. Meiklejohn, Mr R. Richardson, Mr H. Hunt and Major A. Daukes and by many other observers.

This appears to be the first record for Norfolk. Other rarities that year included a dowitcher or red-breasted snipe on October 5th to November 1st and a white-tailed sea eagle on Kelling Heath on December 29th.

1958

Invasion of yellow wagtails; and, among them, ten blue-headed. Coypus, the aquatic rodent from the Argentine, started to build up in numbers. Coypu have already done great damage to the reed beds in Broadland.

1963

During the first three months of this year, very severe weather was experienced. The sea froze in the creeks and floes drifted onshore. I estimate that 95 per cent of bitterns perished through hunger as did the kingfishers, wrens, redwings and fieldfares. Bearded tits managed to survive: they were artificially fed on Cley and reeds were cut to help them find food.

1964

An effort was made to grow pine trees, similar to those at Holkam, on Taylor's Hill. Fifty young trees were planted but they failed to flourish.

The first hide overlooking the north scrape was built on April 12th as black-tailed godwits were showing signs of breeding.

The main hide above the road on the Long Drift was erected on May 22nd and the Pool Hide on July 7th.

1964 was termed a quail year. At least five different birds were heard calling during June.

1965

Estimation of breeding duck other than mallard was fifteen to twenty pairs of gadwall, six pairs garganey, six pairs teal, two pairs wigeon, fifteen to twenty pairs shoveler and ten pairs shelduck. There were also four pairs of snipe.

A black-eared wheatear was found on Granborough Hill at Salthouse on August 30th.

An invasion of waxwings on October 19th and 20th. By then, 150 were in the area, increasing to 300 plus on October 28th.

A family of three otter cubs seen on Cley, November 6th.

1966

Eight thousand bunches of reeds were cut on Cley.

Five species of terns recorded on Arnold's Marsh on June 15th - Arctic, common, sandwich, little and roseate.

Party of American Audubon Society members paid a second visit to the Reserve during May.

Royal Engineers in training used earth-moving machines to make a scrape in front of the North Hide. They were, alas, foiled by bad weather.

Kingfishers were again in evidence for the first time since the severe weather of 1963.

1968

A party of fourteen ruffs (or perhaps reeves!) wintered on the Reserve and the surrounding farmland.

Two pairs of black-tailed godwits were in display and scraping nesting sites on April 27th. Both pairs hatched young but both broods were killed by stoats.

An invasion of nutcrackers came in from the sea during mid-September, probably from Siberia.

1969

Two pairs of black-tailed godwits were on eggs by May 14th but only one young bird reached the flying stage.

A pair of sandwich terns laid eggs and hatched them on Arnold's Marsh, but were not successful in rearing young.

An otter was seen with four cubs early in the morning of June 25th.

Mr W. Brett found a pair of quail with a brood of six young on Cley Hall Farm.

Bitterns returned to the Reserve on August 17th, the first recorded since the severe weather of 1963.

Curlew sandpiper passed through in abnormal numbers. There were literally hundreds of them during September.

Four bluethroats were around the Reserve on September 18th.

Four adult otters were seen playing in the Big Pool on October 1st.

A cream-coloured courser seen in sugar beet field at Blakeney between October 18th and 26th, and longbilled dowitcher spotted on November 1st by Mr P. Westall at Cley.

1970

During severe weather at the beginning of the year we artificially fed the Reserve's bitterns with sprats.

Five species of geese seen on January 8th - fourteen pinkfeet, ten whitefronts, eleven greylag, thirty Canadas and two Egyptian.

Large movement of yellow wagtails during late April. With them were twelve blue-headed.

Three nests of black-tailed godwits on Cley. Only one chick reached the flying stage on June 19th.

1971

Bitterns were again booming on Cley - the first time since the severe weather experienced during early 1963.

Millions of ladybirds invaded the area on August 2nd.

Two young bitterns of the year were observed from one of the hides on August 3rd.

A northerly gale on November 21st and 22nd flooded both Cley and Salthouse marshes to 2 feet above the normal level.

1972

My son, Bernard Bishop, started as assistant warden on Cley Reserve on February 20th.

The pool known as Carter's Scrape was enlarged during late February.

A Chinese water deer was seen around the Big Pool on May 1st. Where had this little animal escaped from?

A pochard's nest with eggs found on Cley Marsh. This nest hatched successfully in late May.

New work began on Cley Marsh when a few generous donors contributed to a pool fund, started by Mr Justin Carter, to increase areas of open mud and water.

A second scrape was started on August 17th and named Simmond's Scrape. The North Scrape was enlarged between August 25th and September 2nd.

1973

Maynard's Hide was erected overlooking the west end of the North Scrape on March 29th.

The Public Hide near the car park was almost completely destroyed by a gale on April 2nd and Maynard's Hide was demolished by the same gale.

A pair of godwits hatched on April 28th and two young birds of this brood reached the flying stage on June 22nd.

Miss Pat Luckett gave a donation to start yet another scrape on what was then known as the Bath Marsh. This was renamed Pat's Pool after her.

Otter cubs were heard around the Big Pool on August 26th.

Wilson's phalarope seen on Carter's Scrape on October 21st.

1974

Pintail resting on Cley in larger numbers. Over 200 were present on January 7th.

Avocets are also coming in increasing numbers. On April 14th, twenty-seven were present, the largest number I had ever seen at Cley.

The North Scrape was further improved during July.

A hard northerly gale on September 24th brought in over one hundred Arctic skuas and thirty great skuas.

Little auks were passing offshore on October 28th; over 120 were recorded in two hours.

1975

Avocets mating on June 9th.

A definite decrease in swallows and martins.

On July 26th, twenty-three species of waders reported on the Reserve.

Irene Hide erected during the first week of October.

Many more hen harriers than for years past were present on the Reserve during the later part of the year.

1976

The increase of hen harriers continued.

A purple heron was seen over Salthouse marshes on November 3rd, and a redfooted falcon at Salthouse Heath May 17th.

Many quails were reported in the area and two were calling in the garden of Watcher's Cottage during May.

A great snipe was shot by a local gunner at Salthouse and given to me and is now in Norwich Museum.

A fine specimen of an adult white-winged black tern was feeding over the Cley Reserve on June 6th.

The first British record of a fantail warbler was seen from the East Bank at Cley on August 24th, followed by a Pallas grasshopper warbler on September 13th.

1977

The successful breeding of two pairs of avocets was the most notable event of 1977 at Cley Reserve. Six young were reared to flying stage.

The first three months of the year were very mild, resulting in an early migration of summer visitors.

Another white-winged black tern put in an appearance from June 2nd to June 9th.

The resident flock of brent geese increased to around two thousand feeding daily on the Eye field.

1978

On January 4th, yet another surge of sea water flooded the Reserve to a depth of 2 feet above normal.

A much colder early spring than the previous year resulted in a later migration.

A black stork, a wanderer from eastern Europe, came in from the sea on April 28th, a new addition to the county list.

Avocets increased to five pairs and reared a total of seventeen young.

A little bittern appeared on August 5th and 6th.

The second county record of a desert wheatear was found on the beach on October 14th.

1979

A local roost of hen harriers increased to fifteen birds during the early part of the year.

A purple heron was seen from May 16th to 26th and a rose-coloured starling from May 19th to 27th.

A black-headed gull was seen by several observers to take the full brood of a black-tailed godwit on May 27th.

There was a marsh sandpiper on Simmond's Scrape from August 14th to 18th.

A public hide was opened in memory of Richard Richardson who was a very well known bird artist and ornithologist and had died the previous year.

A little bittern was seen on May 20th and a little egret on May 30th, as well as a Wilson's phalarope in full plumage on Richardson's Scrape on May 17th to 18th, and a blackheaded bunting from April 30th to May 3rd.

1980

One thousand four hundred brent geese were feeding daily on the Reserve during January and early February.

A new hide was opened in memory of a well known ornithologist, Godfrey Whitwell, on August 2nd.

Avocets increased in numbers of breeding pairs to twenty.

Among rare birds seen were a purple heron and a caspian tern on August 26th; one white-rumped sandpiper was reported on August 2nd, two on August 12th and another on October 30th to November 2nd. Sardinian warbler, the second county record, was seen from September 2nd to October 5th.

During very heavy thunder storms on August 7th 4.14 inches of rain was recorded by a local farmer, Mr J. Case of Cockthorpe.

1981

1981 was the wettest year for two decades.

One hundred and sixteen barnacle geese were resting on the Blakeney Marshes during March.

Twenty six pairs of avocets bred at Cley.

A new visitors' centre was opened on July 6th, overlooking the Reserve in memory of a very well known naturalist and broadcaster, the late R.P. Bagnall-Oakeley.

The resident wintering flock of brent geese increased to 2,000. Three avocets' nests were flooded by heavy rain on May 27th, but despite this thirty-five young were reared to the flying stage.

A white-rumped sandpiper on July 6th and another on August 6th.

The first accepted British record of a rock sparrow was recorded at Cley on June 6th.

*Extracts from the Warden's
Diary 1982 - 1996*
Bernard Bishop

1982

Much increased number of Pintail moving between Cley and Blakeney Harbour during January and February - as many as 1000.

A party of 6 Red-necked Grebes offshore on January 26th.

A rare spring occurrence of a Spotted Crake in the last week of April; a Corncrake in early May was the first record in the area for many years.

Rare waders included Buff-breasted, Terek and Broad-billed Sandpipers in May, and only the second recorded Marsh Sandpiper in mid-July.

Most Snow Geese seen locally are almost certainly escapes from collections, but a party of 12 that rested overnight on the Reserve on September 21st after strong westerlies could well have been genuine wild vagrants.

A total of 16 Bean Geese on the Reserve on November 6th.

1983

Gale force north-easterlies continued for over a week in early February bringing onshore huge numbers of dead and dying seabirds, the vast majority of them Auk species. This 'wreck' extended all down the eastern coasts of England and Scotland. A total of 6500 birds were counted in Norfolk (more than any other county) and the RSPB recorded more than 500 dead birds between Weybourne and Blakeney Point, the majority of them Razorbills and Guillemots with smaller numbers of Little Auks, Puffins and other species.

At the end of February work on enlarging North Scrape was completed, with the intention of extending suitable breeding habitat for Avocets in quieter parts of the Reserve. In the six years since 1977 numbers of breeding pairs have steadily increased to 26, with 55 young successfully reared last year.

Six Spoonbills took up residence for a week at the end of April and 3 or 4 stayed in the area for much of the summer.

The last few days of May were eventful! On the 22nd two Bee-eaters were seen at Blakeney and at Cley and a Spotted Sandpiper in summer plumage arrived on the Reserve. This was followed by a Night Heron

WARDEN'S DIARY 1982-1996

which flew into the reedbeds in the evening. It remained in the area until June 2nd, roosting during the day in Wiveton Hall woods and flying onto the Reserve each evening where it was watched by large numbers of birders.

There was another addition to the Cley list on 28th when a Cattle Egret flew in from the east, departing in the evening.

But it was the autumn that produced the rarity of the year. On August 9th a Lesser Crested Tern was identified among Sandwich terns on Blakeney Point (the first record for England). It was seen fishing offshore and periodically frequented Arnold's Marsh for over a month, finally departing in mid-September.

1984

About 150 Barnacle Geese present during the last week of January. Such numbers are very rarely seen at Cley.

On March 13th, 72 Bewick's Swans were counted on the Reserve.

Conversion of Billy's hide for use by the disabled was completed. It was officially reopened on March 21st. This hide (on the south side of the Coast Road overlooking Carter's Scrape) was one of the first to be built on the Reserve in 1964. For many years it was used for meeting visitors and selling permits, and Father regularly met his pals there on Sunday mornings when the talk was as much about football and the fortunes of Norwich City as it was about birds. And with an audience to play to he was not above making fun of any visitor who wanted to know if any rarities were about before buying a permit, rather than simply wanting to enjoy the Reserve.

A Dipper on Snipe's Marsh on April 7th was the first record at Cley for many years. A week later a White Stork on the Reserve, seen at several points along the coast in the next few days.

May brought persistent north easterlies, and on 9th one of those vagrants that attracts birders from far and wide. A Ross's Gull in summer plumage was spotted in late morning on Arnold's Marsh - a long way from its breeding grounds in N.E. Siberia. At least 40 people arrived within the hour and more than 150 by the end of the day. Over the weekend it was seen at Blakeney Point and again over Arnold's Marsh and North Scrape, drawing another 300 visitors to the Reserve.

Mid-August saw the arrival of a Marsh Sandpiper which stayed for about 3 weeks.

An exceptional movement of 2500 Kittiwakes eastwards on November 4th.

1985

A very cold start to the year - ice-floes appeared offshore in January. These very harsh conditions resulted in some unusual movements mid-month: 1000 Knot and 120 Scaup were seen flying west on 15th; a score of Smew and Goosander offshore on 17th; and about 25 Woodcock appeared at Marsh Lane on 19th.

A sudden rush of migrants in early April included an Alpine Swift on 3rd. May brought an influx of Bluethroats. 28 were recorded over a period of a fortnight, mainly along Blakeney Point, but including a few individuals of the Red-spotted race at Cley.

A Marsh warbler singing by Cley Bank in early June was the first record of this species since the 1920's.

A summer irruption of Crossbills, with up to 14 seen at Cley between July 9th and 22nd. They were joined on 17th and 18th by an adult Parrot Crossbill with 4 juveniles (a pair had bred at Wells for the second year running).

A Greater Sandplover appeared at the end of July, only the second county record. It remained for the month of August ensuring the hides were crammed with a constant stream of visitors.

This was nothing, however, to the havoc caused on August 24th by the arrival of a Little Whimbrel. This tiny, delicate bird nests in Siberia, migrating south through central Asia, and its presence as far west as Norfolk gave birders the chance of a lifetime. So many descended on the area, they were sleeping in church porches, bus shelters, barns and pub floors. Even 'The Times' reported on this invasion.

A White-billed Diver offshore near Halfway House on September 29th - a county first.

November was very cold. Unusually large movements of Pomerine Skuas in the first half of the month - 100+ on the 2nd and 200 on the 10th were peak numbers.

A Great Grey Shrike overwintered on Salthouse Heath.

1986

In early January a Red-breasted Goose was spotted in a large flock of Brents (an addition to the Cley list). Upwards of 40 White-fronts on the Reserve during January and February.

An influx of continental Mealy Redpolls in March, and a huge 'fall' of about 400 Yellow Wagtails on the Eye Field towards the end of April.

A commemorative lunch was held at 'The George and Dragon' on March 14th by descendants and relatives of the eight naturalists, led by Dr Sidney Long, who had met sixty years earlier to the day at what was then the George Hotel. Over lunch on that day in 1926 the eight men discussed proposals for the future of the marsh which Dr Long had purchased the week before for £5100. This meeting led to the establishment of the Reserve and the founding of the Norfolk Naturalists Trust.

The 60th Anniversary of the Trust was celebrated on May 31st with an Open Day on the Reserve. Craft tents and stands were erected on the Eye Field, tractors and trailers ferried people down to the hides, and guided walks were led by Ted Ellis, Michael Seago and Don Dorling. The event was opened by Bill Oddie. He recalled how much he'd enjoyed coming to Cley as a child, and how he would try to keep out of Father's way to avoid paying for a permit! Despite incessant rain all day, hundreds of visitors made the event a great success.

May was otherwise uneventful, but June brought a very rare sighting of a Spotted Sandpiper. Avocets had a very successful breeding season. The number of pairs rearing young increased to over 50. A pair of Black Redstarts bred near Salthouse.

Large numbers of Manx and Sooty Shearwaters offshore after strong north winds in early September.

Very large passage of Little Gulls from mid-October to the end of November. Also large movements of Kittiwakes and Little Auks at the beginning of November.

A long-staying Dotterel appeared on November 9th and remained, mainly on the Eye Field, until the new year.

Father's death on September 3rd drew many handsome tributes to his achievements over a lifetime devoted to the Reserve.

1987

Sightings of Red Kite flying over at the end of February - the first to be seen in the area for some years.

A Red-rumped Swallow around the village from April 8th - 12th caused traffic jams in the High Street.

Rare spring migrants mid-month included Alpine Swift and Hoopoe. Another large 'fall' of Yellow Wagtails on the Eye Field, and a Stone Curlew on the Reserve at the end of the month.

The highlight of the year was the appearance of a pair of Slender-billed Gulls on May 12th. They were observed displaying and mating (mainly around North Scrape) but departed after four days. A busy time dealing with a huge number of visitors.

Other notable May arrivals included Wilson's Phalarope, a singing male Savi's Warbler and a Rustic Bunting near the Mill. Good numbers of Bluethroats at the end of the month.

An American Wigeon at the end of June and a Blue-winged Teal (another N. American vagrant and a new species for Cley) seen in September. A Caspian Tern on August 20th.

An Olive-backed Pipit and Dusky Warbler on successive days along Blakeney Point in the first week of October (strong south-easterlies).

The 'Great Storm' mid-month thankfully left North Norfolk relatively unscathed. The Reserve suffered no damage.

Following Father's death, an appeal was launched to fund a memorial of some kind, commemorating his lifetime's work at Cley. He had always been keen to encourage Black-tailed Godwit to nest on the Reserve on a regular basis, and so it was decided to create a new wet area or 'washland' in his memory. This involved digging out an area of grazing marsh stretching from Simmond's Scrape, north to the Main Drain and eastwards almost to North Scrape. This digging work was completed in October and we were able to get fresh water onto this part of the marsh for the first time.

1988

A Red-breasted Goose that appeared in December remained in the area with flocks of Brents until the beginning of March.

An unusual widespread movement of Red Kites around the county began mid-March. One was seen at Cley on the 12th.

A rare spring record of a Spotted Crake at the end of April when one was heard calling at night.

Frequent east winds during May brought two species new to the area - Bonelli's Warbler and Thrush Nightingale (both on Blakeney Point). Mid-month a Little Egret on the Reserve - the first for several years.

Highlight of the summer was a singing male Great Reed Warbler in the main reedbeds and around Irene Hide for most of June.

At the end of August a Lesser Crested Tern on Arnold's Marsh - only the second occurrence at Cley. A very rare sighting of a Bee-eater on the Reserve on September 3rd and 4th. A White-rumped sandpiper at the end of the month was the only rare wader this year.

October rarities include Pied Wheatear and Radde's Warbler on Blakeney Point and a Black-eared Wheatear at Salthouse.

Five Yellow-browed Warblers were seen during the month. They seem to be becoming an annual autumn event. A Siberian Stonechat at Coastguards was only the third local record.

One of the biggest influxes of Waxwings I can remember began on October 30th. Forty or so were seen around Cley and Wiveton over the next few days. Large numbers were reported all down the east coast.

In December Nancy Gull retired and 'Nancy's Cafe', renowned throughout the birding world, closed down. For more than 20 years the Cafe was *the* meeting place for visiting birders, and once the telephone was installed in the mid-1970's, a sort of unofficial information centre - these were the days before pagers and mobile phones were a standard part of a 'twitcher's' equipment. During May and the autumn months the phone just never stopped ringing - and a phone call would sometimes empty the cafe in seconds, leaving cups of tea and unfinished meals abandoned at the tables. The end of an era.

1989

A flock of 1000 Pink-feet on New Year's day.

A heavy passage of about 1000 Curlew on April 20th.

Semi-palmated Sandpiper on North Scrape for 3 days in mid-May - the first local record of this North American vagrant since 1953. A few days later a Thrush Nightingale singing at Walsey Hills.

Mid-June a Red-footed Falcon around Wiveton Hall, and a Purple Heron flying west.

Marsh Harriers bred locally for the first time, nesting on Pope's Marsh and rearing four young of which three were strikingly patterned with white. Water Rails also bred. They may do so more often than we think but their retiring habits make it difficult to be certain. Several pairs of Quail also bred in the locality.

Large passage of seabirds in the last week of August: more than 1200 Manx Shearwaters, 2000 Gannets and 100+ Arctic and Great Skuas, all on the 27th. Also 400 Whimbrel at Salthouse the same day.

A dozen or so Water Pipits appeared at the end of October and overwintered on the Reserve for the first time.

200+ Eider passed westwards on November 18th.

1990

Overwintering Water Pipits increased to 20+ during February.

A Green-winged Teal in mid-February and again from late March to the end of April. Also for a few days in mid-March an American Wigeon.

A White Stork at various points along the coast in early April - seen moving between Cley and Blakeney on 10th.

A massive influx of 1000+ Black Terns mid-morning on May 2nd. The view from Irene Hide was one I shall never forget. They flew in low in hundreds towards the hide, and you could clearly hear the clicking of their bills as they snapped at insects. They stayed over the marsh until late afternoon. A superb sight.

The first week of the month also saw an unusually heavy passage of waders, particularly Ruff (150 or so on the Reserve). Notable also in May were a singing male Savi's Warbler, a Night Heron on Pope's Marsh and a Red-footed Falcon which appeared at the end of June.

Two pairs of White-fronted Geese bred successfully.

A Blue-winged Teal on North Scrape towards the end of June, staying on well into July and attracting a stream of birders. More 'attractions' in August: White-rumped, Pectoral and Broad-billed Sandpipers and Norfolk's second record of a Pacific Golden Plover.

A Penduline Tit seen near the Windmill on October 13th was a first for the area. But the event of the month was a massive 'fall' that began on the 18th, when thousands of Redwing, Fieldfare and Blackbirds arrived along the coast. There were also notable numbers of Song Thrush, Robins, Goldcrests and Ring Ouzels. An Olive-backed Pipit was found on Blakeney Point and a number of Arctic Redpolls were seen over the next few days, together with a Dusky Warbler at Gramborough Hill.

Another influx of Water Pipits towards the end of the month.

A very large number of Pintail present during November - estimates of around 1700.

1991

A quiet spring, enlivened by the appearance of a Snowy Owl on Blakeney Point in late March - the first Norfolk record for many decades - and a Sardinian Warbler on Muckleborough Hill in the last week of April.

July and August were exceptionally hot and dry. Reduced water levels on the marsh provided the opportunity to carry out improvement work, particularly on Pat's Pool.

White-rumped Sandpiper at the beginning of August for the second year running.

Large autumn movements of Long-tailed, Pomarine and Great Skuas, particularly on September 29th and 30th when over 1000 Kittiwakes were seen moving west.

A migrant Goshawk was spotted on October 6th, the first Cley record in ten years; a Short-toed Lark near North Hide mid-month; and a unique offshore sighting of a Surf Scoter on 20th in a massive movement of Common Scoters that continued over the next few days.

An influx of Long-eared Owls at the end of October. Six were seen at Cley on 27th.

In late November flooded fields in the Glaven Valley held well in excess of 300 Snipe.

Pacific Golden Plover again on the Reserve in the first week of December.

1992

An unusually large number of Mediterranean Gulls were reported from March onwards. A pair nested for the first time on Blakeney Point but they failed to rear young. This was the first breeding record for the county.

A warm May with S.E. winds brought a flood of rarities. The month began with two new species for Cley: a Ring-billed Gull on Pat's Pool and a Serin identified flying over. Also during the first week, a Little Egret, a species that is becoming a much more regular visitor. Two days later a Glossy Ibis - the first sighting at Cley for 40 years.

Weather conditions on 14th and 15th brought in migrants travelling far to the west of their usual routes north. They included five Red-footed Falcons over Cley and Blakeney and 10 Grey-headed Wagtails in the Eye Field together with Red-throated Pipit. Also good numbers of Black Terns on the Reserve.

May ended with another addition to the Cley list - a Lesser Yellowlegs in summer plumage on 28th and 29th.

The first record of a Marsh Warbler for some years on June 11th.

Yet another bird new to Cley on July 29th when a Red-necked Stint was identified near North Hide - a county first and only the second British record of this vagrant from eastern Siberia. Followed a few days later by a Greater Sand Plover.

A strong autumn passage of Black Terns: 300+ on September 11th.

1993

A remarkable spring and early summer began in the last week of April with the first record of a Sociable Plover at Cley followed a couple of days later by a Great White Egret. Both birds were present for several days also visiting sites further west along the coast.

At the end of May a Desert Warbler at the Hood was observed over six days singing and nest-building - a county first and the first British spring record.

On May 30th the number of birders converging on Cley increased dramatically when a Pacific Swift was identified over North Scrape. During the course of the day, the whole village actually came to a standstill - cars weren't so much parked, they were simply abandoned; people were running and charging about everywhere. When the bird moved over towards the Coast Road, Old Woman's Lane became blocked, and you couldn't get a car in or out of the village. It disappeared about 4.00 p.m. but less fortunate birders were still arriving well into the evening. A first British onshore record - the only previous sighting had been on a North Sea gas platform.

Five days later an Oriental Pratincole that had first been seen inland at Gimingham in mid-May appeared at Halfway House for a couple of hours before heading west. Another Cley first and only the third British record.

Egyptian Geese bred on the Reserve for the first time. A Bewick's Swan took up residence in July and stayed throughout the summer. Presumably it was sick or injured.

Autumn rarities included Broad-billed and Buff-breasted Sandpipers and Arctic and Cetti's Warblers.

A massive 'fall' of migrant Wheatears, Redstarts, Pied Flycatchers and Winchats in mid-September; a notable westward movement of Siskins on October 15th.

1994

A big eastward movement of Guillemot/Razorbills on February 20th. About 2000 during the day.

Large numbers of Black-tailed Godwit during April, peaking at an estimated 780 on 16th - quite a sight.

A singing male Great Reed Warbler around Richardson's Hide on May 11th. Stayed on the Reserve until the end of June, often near the Beach Road.

Also in May: a Blue-winged Teal, Lesser Yellowlegs, two Whiskered Tern on Pat's Pool (the first local record of these really elegant birds for many years), and a singing Scarlet Rosefinch.

Marsh harriers successfully bred on the Reserve.

A Collared Pratincole made its first appearance in the county this century, moving between Cley and Titchwell for most of July.

Large offshore movement of Skuas on September 1st.

An Aquatic Warbler at the Half-moon Pool on October 11th.

A county-wide invasion of Rough-legged Buzzards in the second half of the month. Three were in the Cley area between October 23rd and 30th.

White-winged Black Tern and Desert Wheatear during the first week of November, followed by a Red-rumped Swallow over the village for three days.

1995

A Little Egret in the flooded Glaven meadows near the village green in the first week of February.

14 Bewick's Swans on Arnold's Marsh on March 14th - took off joining another 18 moving east. Flocks of this size are most unusual on spring passage.

A Collared Flycatcher reported near the East Bank on May 5th - a new bird for Cley and only the second county record. Another new species for the area on June 1st when a Laughing Gull (North American vagrant), first spotted at Salthouse, was later seen on the Reserve and in Blakeney Harbour.

A huge build-up of Kittiwakes along the coast in the last week of June after a period of persistent northerly winds. Many thousands were reported between Cromer and Blakeney Point, with at least 1000 off Cley Beach on 27th.

A Collared Pratincole for the second year running from July 4th to 6th and again from 14th to 23rd. An unprecedented 23 Mediterranean Shearwaters on 9th and 10th flying east with Common Scoters.

A large 'fall' of migrants on September 18th with very large numbers of Redstarts, Wheatears, Pied Flycatchers and Willow Warblers along the coast.

The 'Dr Sidney Long Appeal' was launched by Norfolk Wildlife Trust to raise funds for new hides and boardwalks, and for other improvements to the Reserve. On September 26th, work began with the dismantling of Avocet, Daukes, Richardson's and Maynard's Hides.

On October 10th an enormous Leather-backed Turtle was watched for an hour offshore in a sea as flat as a millpond. Perhaps its appearance has something to do with the very long, hot summer.

A Spotted Crake on the Big Pool on 17th attracted a large audience.

A record 300 Little Auks passing offshore on October 29th was surpassed on November 2nd when at least 1200 were counted during the day. Movements of smaller numbers continued through the month.

The displacement of such large numbers was thought to be the result of unusually severe weather off Iceland.

Several thousand disoriented Pink-footed Geese circling overhead at night in heavy fog on November 13th. 500 were reported landing on a road near Fakenham!

Many sightings of Arctic Redpolls from mid-November to mid-December.

Extraordinary to find a Quail near Bittern Hide on November 15th. It remained in the same small area until Boxing Day, when it presumably perished.

1996

High tides and north easterly winds on February 19th and 20 brought devastation to the Reserve.

Work on the new visitor facilities had progressed well over the winter. The boardwalks had been completed. Both Daukes and Avocet Hides were built and thatching had begun.

On the 19th the shingle bank east of Coastguards took a severe battering and a good deal of water was lying on the marsh. Water was lapping over the boardwalk but it was just possible to reach the hides wearing Wellington boots. Some sections of the boardwalk were just afloat but, optimistically, I thought that if things got no worse we might escape serious damage.

But by mid-afternoon blizzards were driving from the east, and at Salthouse the sea had broken through the shingle bank. By the evening the whole of Salthouse Marsh was under several feet of water which was lapping over the East Bank. The only way for that water to drain off was through Cley Marsh, and it is true to say that I went to bed that night with some misgivings.

I was not, however, prepared for the scene next morning. When I looked through the window just before daylight I could not, at first, work out where everything had gone. It was not until I got out and walked around that the scale of the devastation sank in.

The East Bank had been breached overnight and the enormous volume of water to the east had completely inundated the marsh. Seawater was now lapping just below the top of the West Bank and the Coast Road was submerged from the village eastwards. The boardwalk was floating in sections all down the southern edge of the floodwater, along with uprooted bridges, gates and the remnants of hides. 1800 bundles of reed that had been stacked near the central hides in readiness for thatching were washed down towards the village and were completely ruined. Everything was clogged with thousands of tons of reed debris.

Teal and Irene Hides had been demolished and were washed away; Pool Hide remained intact but was 70 or 80 yards away from where it should have been; Bittern Hide had been damaged but not beyond repair, while North Hide, being on higher ground, suffered relatively little. The new hides, firmly bolted to their concrete bases, had stood up fairly well.

Though there was, naturally, a fear that the entire development plan might have to be abandoned, we quickly decided to press ahead despite the enormous setback, and though it was to take almost three weeks for the floodwaters to drain off, clearing up operations began within a few days. The Trust launched a Disaster Appeal which drew a wonderful response from the public. In due course we were able to organise teams of volunteers and, amongst many others, members of the Cley Bird Club did sterling work.

It is a tribute to all those people that the official opening by the Prince of Wales took place, as planned, on March 28th.

The effects of saltwater flooding on the vegetation and wildlife were, of course, also considerable. The freshwater fish stocks, mainly Roach and Rudd, were completely destroyed, depriving many species, including the Bittern, of their food supply. Much of the grass on the grazing marshes was killed off, posing a threat to ground-nesting birds such as the Lapwing and Redshank.

While the reed-beds were under water, Bearded Tits were to be found mainly on Snipe's Marsh, and Water Rails, normally so secretive, were foraging in the debris along the Coast Road. Both of these species quickly returned to the Reserve as the water receded.

Once the water-level had dropped sufficiently, the banks of all the scrapes and dykes were broken to allow saltwater to run off. They were then flushed through with fresh water, and once the Environment Agency were satisfied with the results of their salinity tests, we were able to renew the fish stocks.

Thankfully, Bitterns returned within a few weeks and by the spring they were once again booming on the Reserve.

As the year progressed, the foundations were laid for Teal Hide, and the base was put down for a new hide to replace Irene Hide. The Trust announced that this is to be named Bishop's Hide in recognition of the family's involvement with Cley Marsh Reserve throughout the 70 years of its history. I count that a great honour.

Birds of Cley

Billy Bishop's notes from the first edition have been retained, except for minor changes to reflect current classification. *Additional notes on records since then follow in italics.*

Pashley and Richardson, mentioned in this list, are references to two editions of *The Birds of Cley*. The original edition by H.N. Pashley was published in 1925; it was revised and updated in 1962 by Richard Richardson.

CHECKLIST

Red-throated Diver *(Gavia stellata)*
Winter visitor and passage migrant in fair numbers off-shore, mostly in autumn.

Black-throated Diver *(Gavia arctica)*
Scarce winter visitor - not so many as formerly by any means.

Great Northern Diver *(Gavia immer)*
Scarce winter visitor, met with in the harbour during severe weather.
Singles are seen offshore occasionally.

White-billed Diver *(Gavia adamsii)*
Very rare vagrant. Just two local records in 1985 and 1986.

Little Grebe *(Tachybaptus ruficollis)*
Common breeding bird and visitor to pools away from the coast.
Frequently to be found on the Reserve in the main drain.

Great Crested Grebe *(Podiceps cristatus)*
Breeds outside the area.
Often to be seen in small groups offshore an autumn and winter.

Red-necked Grebe *(Podiceps grisegena)*
Scarce but regular winter visitor, particularly in severe weather when the Baltic is frozen.

Slavonian Grebe *(Podiceps auritus)*
Scarce but regular visitor to Blakeney Harbour.
Also occasionally offshore in small numbers.

Black-necked Grebe *(Podiceps nigricollis)*
Scarce and irregular winter visitor.

Fulmar *(Fulmarus glacialis)*
Regular visitor along the coast. Breeds in small numbers at Weybourne.
Cliff erosion is adversely affecting the Weybourne colony.

Cory's Shearwater *(Calonectris diomedea)*
Rare vagrant. There have been a dozen or so records over the past few years.

Great Shearwater *(Puffinus gravis)*
Rare visitor, chiefly in the autumn. Seen singly at Cley August 14th and 15th 1896, October 29th 1939 and September 2nd 1960.
Since then, there have been three records, most recently in September 1973.

Sooty Shearwater *(Puffinus griseus)*
Now a regular autumn visitor.
Seen mainly in August and September. The largest count was 150 on September 3rd 1986.

Manx Shearwater *(Puffinus puffinus)*
Regular migrant on passage.
Counts of up to 250 have been recorded.

Mediterranean or **Yelkouan Shearwater** *(Puffinus yelkouan)*
Scarce and irregular autumn visitor. First recorded in this area at Blakeney Point on September 22nd 1891. Pashley refers to it as a Western Mediterranean Shearwater
Known in my father's time as the 'Balearic Shearwater', and considered at that time a race of the Manx Shearwater. It is recorded fairly regularly in small numbers, mainly in August or September. A record count of 23 on July 9th and 10th 1995.

Little Shearwater *(Puffinus assimilis)*
Rare visitor (Madeiran race). One dead at Blakeney Point on May 11th 1929 and another at Blakeney Point on May 1st 1960.

Storm Petrel *(Hydrobates pelagicus)*
Scarce visitor to inshore waters except when storm driven.
Only nine recorded occurrences since 1970.

Leach's Petrel *(Oceanodroma leucorhoa)*
Scarce visitor. Hardly ever seen except when storm driven to coastal waters.
Commoner than the Storm Petrel. Most records in late autumn on passage.

Gannet *(Sula bassana)*
Seen often in good numbers, more so when mackerel are offshore in late summer.
Largest numbers (300 - 400) coincide with autumn northerly winds.

CHECKLIST

Cormorant *(Phalacrocorax carbo)*
Regular visitor to inland pools and coastal waters.
Flocks of 30 or so can sometimes be seen on the North Scrape.

Shag *(Phalacrocorax aristotelis)*
Occasional visitor to harbour and local ponds.
Usually seen in winter and on passage.

Bittern *(Botaurus stellaris)*
Regular breeding bird in small numbers. Very cold winters severely affect them. I found the first bittern's nest ever recorded in 1937. There were at least three nests in reedbeds in 1980.
One or two pairs have continued to breed most years. In 1995 Norfolk Wildlife Trust, in association with other organisations, implemented a programme of reed-bed management aimed at encouraging further breeding.

Little Bittern *(Ixobrychus minutus)*
Rare visitor to reed beds. Seen singly at Cley on July 26th and November 6th 1952, August 7th to 24th 1956, August 26th 1958, October 27th 1970, August 5th and 6th 1978 and May 20th 1979.

Night Heron *(Nycticorax nycticorax)*
Rare visitor. One at Weybourne on July 17th 1887, and one at Stiffkey on May 30th 1976.
More recently, an adult at Cley from May 23rd to June 2nd 1983. It was seen each evening over the Reserve, flying in from its roost in Wiveton Hall Woods. Also an adult seen at Salthouse and on Pope's Marsh May 10th 1990.

Cattle Egret *(Bubulcus ibis)*
One record only; an adult on May 28th 1983.

Little Egret *(Egretta garzetta)*
Rare spring visitor. Seen singly at Cley May 7th to 10th 1952, May/June 1953, April/May 1955, June 15th to 19th 1966, a series of records from April 30th to July 12th 1972, and May 30th 1979.
There have been further irregular occurrences, including another unusual series of records between April and August 1994. One was also present at Stiffkey over the winter of 1995/6.

CLEY MARSH AND ITS BIRDS

Great White Egret *(Egretta alba)*
A single bird was recorded on the Reserve - April 26th to May 3rd 1993.

Grey Heron *(Ardea cinerea)*
Common breeding species. Small heronries at Cley Hall farm and Wiveton Hall.
Migrating flocks can occasionally be seen in the autumn.

Purple Heron *(Ardea purpurea)*
Spring visitors in small numbers. Pashley does not record any. Seen singly at Cley May 10th to 12th 1951, May 11th 1957 and May 9th 1959.
Irregular sightings have continued, mainly in May, many of them immatures.

Black Stork *(Ciconia nigra)*
Rare visitor seen singly at Salthouse on August 23rd 1888, at Cley on September 20th 1901, two at Blakeney September 17th and 18th 1905, and one at Cley April 28th 1978.

White Stork *(Ciconia ciconia)*
Rare visitor seen near Holt 1836, Cley 1849, Salthouse mid-1880, Cley August 19th and 20th 1891 and Morston June 4th 1953.
There have been four isolated records since. The most recent was on Blakeney Fresh Marshes April 10th to 12th 1990.

Glossy Ibis *(Plegadis falcinellus)*
Rare visitor to tidal waters. This is a bird I have never personally seen in this area. Five were recorded on October 20th 1891, three on June 17th 1893, five in August 1898, one on November 5th 1921 and one on September 24th 1952.
One was also seen on May 6th 1992 on the Reserve and at Kelling.

Spoonbill *(Platalea leucorodia)*
Scarce but regular summer visitors to both Cley and Salthouse Marshes. More regular in recent years
Groups of up to six may be seen most years between April and August.

Flamingo *(Phoenicopterus ruber)*
These birds show up full winged periodically but must be accepted as escapes from ornamental collections either in this country or on the continent.

CHECKLIST

Mute Swan *(Cygnus olor)*
Breeding resident in small numbers.

Bewick's Swan *(Cygnus columbianus)*
As with whooper swan, regular passage migrant to the Fens and winter visitor.
Mostly seen on passage west in late autumn/winter when flocks of up to 50 have been recorded; much less frequently in spring. Uniquely, one stayed on the Reserve from July 3rd to mid-September 1994.

Whooper Swan *(Cygnus cygnus)*
Scarce but regular passage migrant and winter visitor.
Occurs in small numbers, but by no means every year.

Bean Goose *(Anser fabalis)*
Scarce winter visitor.

Pink-footed Goose *(Anser brachyrhynchus)*
Regular winter visitor. Before the anti-aircraft firing range was built at Stiffkey just prior to the Second World War, many thousand rested daily in Blakeney Harbour.
Back on the increase in the area. Several thousand roost at Wells and Scolt Head, and large numbers can be heard flying overhead some winter mornings; also at night, especially in fog.

White-fronted Goose *(Anser albifrons)*
Regular passage migrant and winter visitor.
Up to 40 or 50 have been recorded in recent years. A few have also remained during the summer with one or two pairs breeding annually since 1984.

Lesser White-fronted Goose *(Anser erythropus)*
Rare visitor. One at Cley February 3rd to 8th 1961.

Greylag Goose *(Anser anser)*
Genuine wild birds are scarce winter visitors. Few birds are breeding at Cley and other areas of Norfolk.
Became established at Cley in the 1970s and is now present in large numbers. Flocks of 300 or so may be seen in autumn and winter. Up to 25 pairs have bred in recent years.

Snow Goose *(Anser caerulescens)*
   Rare visitor. One seen January 9th 1909 and six on October 31st 1912.
   Records are now almost annual, but almost certainly relate to the colony at Holkham Hall.

Canada Goose *(Branta canadensis)*
   During the last ten years have increased in the area. A regular winter flock of around two hundred on the Reserve at Cley.
   More recently, present in smaller numbers, commonly around 80. Now breeds on the Reserve.

Barnacle Goose *(Branta leucopsis)*
   Scarce passage migrant and winter visitor.
   Not seen every year. Usually coincides with hard weather. Singles and smaller groups will almost certainly be escapes from waterfowl collections. Flocks of 100+ in March 1981 and January 1984..

Brent Goose *(Branta bernicla)*
   Both dark and pale breasted brent geese are common and often abundant in the local harbour and on Cley and Salthouse Marshes. A winter population of 1,200 - 1,500 is not exceptional.
   Numbers of the dark breasted form have increased in recent years and around 5000 are in the area between October and early April. A few birds regularly stay for the summer (mainly around Blakeney Harbour). Large numbers may also be seen offshore on passage to wintering grounds further west. A handful of the pale breasted form are present most years.

Red-breasted Goose *(Branta ruficollis)*
   Very rare vagrant. Two records of single adults with Brents in January 1986 and between December 1987 and early March 1988.

Egyptian Goose *(Alopochen aegyptiacus)*
   Occasional visitor presumably from feral stock at Holkham. Breeds on Norfolk coast.
   Sixteen were seen on the Reserve on September 25th 1989 and a pair bred in 1993.

Ruddy Shelduck *(Tadorna ferruginea)*
   Rare visitor. Difficult to prove that they are genuine wild birds as so many are now kept in captivity.

Shelduck *(Tadorna tadorna)*
Common breeding resident.
Counts are highest in early summer when around 300 non-breeding adults are present in the area. Numbers build up again in autumn and early winter as birds return from their moulting grounds in the Waddezee area. North Scrape and Arnold's Marsh hold large numbers of young birds in late summer.

Mandarin Duck *(Aix galericulata)*
These ducks are kept in ornamental ponds and collections and must be accepted as escapes, though these ducks do breed wild in parts of England, e.g. Surrey.

Wigeon *(Anas penelope)*
Common passage migrant and winter visitor. The odd pair is known to breed on the Cley Reserve. Numbers build up in December to around six thousand since Cley became a non-shooting area.
Though numbers fluctuate, they have further increased in recent years. As many as 11,000 may be present in early winter, moving between Cley and Blakeney Harbour.

American Wigeon *(Anas americana)*
Rare visitor. One at Cley November 4th 1969.
There have been only three further sporadic records, most recently March 14th - 18th 1990.

Falcated Duck *(Anas facata)*
Single drakes were on the Reserve associating with Wigeon in May 1988 and 1989. Almost certainly escapes.

Gadwall *(Anas strepera)*
A rare duck twenty-five years ago but are now a quite common breeding resident.
Flocks of 100 or so can be seen from time to time.

Teal *(Anas crecca)*
Common passage migrant and winter visitor. The odd pair have nested on Cley Reserve. The most abundant duck during October.
An estimated 2000 may be present in autumn and early winter. A few pairs now regularly breed.

Green-winged Teal *(Anas crecca carolinensis)*
Rare visitor. One at Cley April 6th 1964.
Males of this North American vagrant have been recorded in spring on a few occasions since.

Mallard *(Anas platyrhynchos)*
Very common breeding resident.

Pintail *(Anas acuta)*
Passage migrant and winter visitor in small numbers. The odd pair breed on the Reserve. They are becoming more common yearly. Four hundred is the biggest number I have known on the Reserve.
There has been a marked increase since my father's day. Winter counts can be well in excess of 1000.

Garganey *(Anas querquedula)*
Summer visitor and passage migrant in small numbers. Up to three pairs breed in the area except the two or three years after a salt-water flood.
Up to five pairs have bred, but usually no more than one or two.

Blue-winged Teal *(Anas discors)*
Very rare migrant. Recorded only three times.

Shoveler *(Anas clypeata)*
Breeding resident in small numbers.
But around 150 usually resident in early winter.

Red-crested Pochard *(Netta rufina)*
Rare visitor. One at Bayfield December 15th 1959 and one at Kelling January 26th 1960.
Records have been almost annual since the mid-eighties, but most are likely to be escapes.

Pochard *(Aythya ferina)*
Passage migrant and winter visitor. Has bred at Cley 1923, 1924, 1929; last breeding date 1973.
Up to 50 regularly winter in the area.

Ferruginous Duck *(Aythya nyroca)*
Rare visitor. One at Cley April 25th and 26th 1958.

CHECKLIST

Tufted Duck *(Aythya fuligula)*
Passage migrant and winter visitor. Has bred regularly at Cley for the past ten years.
A few pairs continue to breed on the Reserve with no more than 50 or so wintering in the area.

Scaup *(Aythya marila)*
Common in severe winters.
Mostly to be seen offshore between September and May (120 were observed flying west in January 1985), but the occasional bird may turn up on Arnold's Marsh.

Common Eider *(Somateria mollissima)*
Seen regularly in small numbers outside Blakeney Harbour.
Numbers seem to have increased and flocks of fifty or so can sometimes be seen offshore. 200 were noted flying westwards in November 1989.

Harlequin Duck *(Histrionicus histrionicus)*
Rare visitor. Seen by myself in a tidal drain sheltering under a wall of ice during very severe weather on February 19th 1947.

Long-tailed Duck *(Clangula hyemalis)*
Winter visitor in small numbers. Seen more regularly in the harbour than a few years back.
Records are mostly of singles offshore or around Arnold's Marsh.

Common Scoter *(Melanitta nigra)*
Common passage migrant outside harbour. Present most of the year.
Rafts of around 1500 can sometimes be seen offshore from October to April. 2000 were observed flying west in October 1991.

Surf Scoter *(Melanitta perspicillata)*
Vagrant. One record of a male flying west on October 20th 1991.

Velvet Scoter *(Melanitta fusca)*
Passage migrant and winter visitor to coastal waters in small numbers.

Goldeneye *(Bucephala clangula)*
Winter visitor and passage migrant; as with scaup duck there are more in hard winters.
Usually to be seen offshore or on Arnold's Marsh.

CLEY MARSH AND ITS BIRDS

Smew *(Mergus albellus)*
Scarce winter visitor, as with goosander, most likely in hard weather.
Mainly singles around Arnold's Marsh. There was a wide-spread influx in January 1985 when 21 were seen at Cley on the 17th.

Red-breasted Merganser *(Mergus serrator)*
Passage migrant and winter visitor. Fairly regular in coastal waters.
Usually to be seen passing offshore. Also to be found in Blakeney Harbour in small numbers.

Goosander *(Mergus merganser)*
Scarce winter visitor; most likely in hard weather.
A few are seen most years. Twenty flying west were recorded on January 17th 1985.

Honey Buzzard *(Pernis apivorus)*
Rare visitor. Less than ten records, last date at Cley September 7th 1979.
Seen sporadically flying over in May/June or autumn. Only six more recent records.

Black Kite *(Milvus migrans)*
Rare visitor. Cley May 14th 1966 (addition to county list) Cley/Salthouse May 6th to 10th 1971, and Cley October 15th 1978.
Further local sightings in July 1985 and April 1993.

Red Kite *(Milvus milvus)*
Rare visitor. Last dates August 13th 1970; March 24th 1973 and Cley December 31st 1978.
Ten more recent records, mostly of singles flying over. Unusually there were several local sightings in March/April 1996.

White-tailed Eagle *(Haliaeetus albicilla)*
Rare winter visitor. Less than ten records including Blakeney Point 1961 and again on December 6th 1962.

Marsh Harrier *(Circus aeruginosus)*
Now a regular spring visitor.
After showing interest for several years, the first pair to breed at Cley nested on Pope's Marsh in 1989 when three of the four young were striking partial albinos. A pair bred on the Reserve in both 1994 and 1995.

CHECKLIST

Hen Harrier *(Circus cyaneus)*
Scarce but regular winter visitor, more so during the last few years, roosting on Kelling Heath. Up to two years ago I had only seen six males in my life, but since then I have seen three times that number.
Now seen fairly regularly between October and April. Small numbers have been known to roost in the Reserve reed-beds in early winter.

Montagu's Harrier *(Circus pygargus)*
As with the Marsh Harrier, a regular spring visitor. Bred on Kelling Heath around 1936.
Recorded most years on passage, often in May.

Goshawk *(Accipiter gentilis)*
Rare visitor. One seen at Weybourne March 9th 1901 and one at Salthouse on June 27th 1952.
Only four more recent records - the last was at Blakeney Fresh Marshes in December 1992.

Sparrowhawk *(Accipiter nisus)*
Not a very common bird but I knew of a breeding pair on Cley Hall Farm from 1969 to 1976.
On the increase. There are now a few regular breeding pairs and individuals can be seen hunting throughout the year.

Common Buzzard *(Buteo buteo)*
Scarce and irregular winter visitor.
No more than one or two are seen most years.

Roughlegged Buzzard *(Buteo lagopus)*
Has become a more regular winter visitor during the last few years.
One or two overwintered in 1985-6. Since then only five records.

Golden Eagle *(Aquila chrysaetos)*
Very rare visitor. One (long dead) found at Stiffkey in November 1868.

Osprey *(Pandion haliaetus)*
These birds are now seen regularly on passage.
Seems to be on the increase. Around ten are now recorded annually.

Kestrel *(Falco tinnunculus)*
Breeds in small numbers; also a passage migrant.

Red-footed Falcon *(Falco vespertinus)*
Rare visitor. Approximately ten have been recorded.
Five more records since, with an exceptional five birds noted May 14th to 15th 1992 (part of a spring total of over 40 in the county).

Merlin *(Falco columbarius)*
Scarce but regular winter visitor.
Two or three birds are seen most winters, often on the Blakeney side, but also over the Reserve.

Hobby *(Falco subbuteo)*
Scarce but regular bird of passage, mostly in autumn.
Has bred in the Cley area.

Gyrfalcon *(Falco rusticolus)*
Rare visitor. December 20th 1953, January 1st to 8th and October 1st 1954.

Peregrine *(Falco peregrinus)*
Scarce but regular bird of passage.
Sightings have increased in recent years - usually single birds flying over between September and April.

Red-legged Partridge *(Alectoris rufa)*
Abundant breeding resident.

Grey Partridge *(Perdix perdix)*
Abundant breeding resident.
But less common than Red-legged Partridge.

Quail *(Coturnix coturnix)*
Irregular summer visitor.
Now recorded almost annually in the area. Remarkably one was present on the Reserve from mid-November to the end of December 1995.

Pheasant *(Phasianus colchicus)*
Abundant breeding resident.

Water Rail *(Rallus aquaticus)*
Much more of a winter visitor than a breeding bird. I have only ever seen one nest, on Salthouse, in 1947.
Breeding was proved on the Reserve in 1989. It may do so more regularly but this is difficult to establish, given its retiring habits.

Spotted Crake *(Porzana porzana)*
Scarce but now regular migrant.
Much less regular these days. The most recent sightings were in August/September 1989 (Carter's Scrape) and in October 1995 (the Big Pool). Water-level management on the Reserve could increase numbers.

Little Crake *(Porzana parva)*
Rare visitor. Second county record this century from September 13th to 24th 1969.

Corncrake *(Crex crex)*
Scarce passage migrant, common at one time. I have only seen two in my life. They are heard more often than seen.
Probably best described as a vagrant. There have been only nine records in the last 35 years.

Moorhen *(Gallinula chloropus)*
Abundant breeding resident.

Coot *(Fulica atra)*
Common breeding resident.

Crane *(Grus grus)*
Very scarce passage migrant. Richardson reports nine records totalling twenty-four birds between 1898 and 1959. One at Cley September 8th 1962, one at Blakeney Point May 3rd 1968, one at Bayfield March 6th to 26th 1979, two at Cley March 17th 1979 and one at Cley May 23rd 1979.
Records most years of birds flying over, mainly in the spring. Most will be from the Broadland colony, but some could well be continental vagrants.

Little Bustard *(Tetrax tetrax)*
The remains of one were found on the Stiffkey Marshes in August 1888.
There was also a single bird recorded at Morston in 1836.

Great Bustard *(Otis tarda)*
The remains of one were found on January 19th 1891, at Stiffkey.

Oyster-catcher *(Haematopus ostralegus)*
A breeding species in fair numbers and a common passage migrant all along the coast.
Breeding pairs have increased. Up to 200 pairs have been recorded in recent years on Blakeney Point.

CLEY MARSH AND ITS BIRDS

Avocet *(Recurvirostra avosetta)*
Pashley describes these birds as rare visitors. Richardson describes them as scarce but regular. They are now breeding and have done so since 1977 and are now fairly established.
Numbers have increased steadily. More than 50 pairs now breed regularly at Cley. Usually present from February to August.

Stone Curlew *(Burhinus oedicnemus)*
The bird is now becoming rare in the area as a breeding bird. Twenty years ago I knew of approximately six regular breeding sites; now I know of none. It sometimes visits the local heathland in autumn.
Nowadays occasionally seen in the area on spring or autumn passage.

Cream Coloured Courser *(Cursorius cursor)*
The fourth county record at Blakeney October 18th to 29th 1969. Picked up dead at Ormesby on November 20th same year and the skin given to the Norwich Castle Museum.

Collared Pratincole *(Glareola pratincola)*
There is a specimen in Norwich Castle Museum, shot at Blakeney in May 1840. One was present on the Reserve from May 4th to July 20th 1994 and again during July 1995.

Oriental Pratincole *(Glareola maldivarum)*
A single record for Norfolk, a bird first recorded near Cromer on May 14th 1993. From there it moved westwards and was seen at Cley and Blakeney on June 4th. It remained on the Norfolk coast until mid-August.

Black-winged Pratincole *(Glareola nordmanni)*
First county record Cley July 3rd to 5th 1966 and Cley August 27th 1974.

Little Ringed Plover *(Charadrius dubius)*
Now a regular visitor in small numbers and has been suspected of breeding.
Now breeds annually (since 1983) in very small numbers. Present from April to September.

Ringed Plover *(Charadrius hiaticula)*
Common breeding bird all along the foreshore and an abundant passage migrant.
Flocks of up to 100 can be seen on the Reserve in spring and autumn.

CHECKLIST

Kentish Plover *(Charadrius alexandrinus)*
Scarce passage migrant to Cley Reserve and coastal marshes.
Mostly seen in April and May and sporadically to September. Breeding has been attempted unsuccessfully.

Greater Sand Plover *(Charadrius leschenaultii)*
An extremely rare vagrant from Southern Russia. Seen on the Reserve July 30th to August 19th 1985, and August 5th to 8th 1992.

Dotterel *(Charadrius morinellus)*
Scarce but regular passage migrant.
Has occurred almost annually over the past 20 years. One remained, mainly around the Eye Field, from November 9th 1986 to January 9th 1987.

Pacific Golden Plover *(Pluvialis fulva)*
Very rare Siberian vagrant that has occurred twice on the Reserve - August 7th and 8th 1990 and December 3rd to 6th 1991.

Golden Plover *(Pluvialis apricaria)*
Winter visitor in moderate numbers to Cley Reserve and surrounding arable land.
Now occurs in most months. Peak numbers in October and November when up to 2000 may be seen, often in the Eye Field.

Grey Plover *(Pluvialis squatarola)*
Winter visitor and passage migrant in moderate numbers. More likely in tidal estuaries.
Mostly to be seen in Blakeney Harbour where up to 1000 may occur in winter.

Sociable Plover *(Chettusia gregaria)*
Very rare vagrant. First record for Cley April 21st to 23rd 1993. This was the fourth record for the county.

Lapwing *(Vanellus vanellus)*
Common breeding species all along the coast, on the marshes and arable land, and a very abundant winter visitor and passage migrant.
Large flocks are regularly seen on the marsh and passing offshore. A count of 3400 on the Reserve January 24th 1989.

Knot *(Calidris canutus)*
An abundant passage migrant and winter visitor. Perhaps the most abundant wader on the East Coast. A few seen in red plumage during spring migration.
Relatively few are to be found on the Reserve (Arnold's Marsh is the most likely spot) but up to 4000 may winter in Blakeney Harbour.

Sanderling *(Calidris alba)*
Regular passage migrant in moderate numbers. A few stay for the winter.
Again, few birds are encountered on the Reserve, while up to 50 can regularly be seen on Blakeney Point.

Semi-palmated Sandpiper *(Calidris pusilla)*
Rare visitor. Cley July 19th to 24th 1953.
A second occurrence May 14th to 17th 1989 on Arnold's Marsh.

Red-necked Stint *(Calidris ruficollis)*
An extremely rare Asian vagrant. An adult on North Scrape July 29th to August 3rd 1992 was a first for Norfolk and only the second British record.

Little Stint *(Calidris minuta)*
Regular passage migrant in varying numbers.
Occurs annually on spring passage in small numbers, mostly in May. In autumn numbers are often larger (up to 100) but more irregular.

Temminck's Stint *(Calidris temminckii)*
Scarce but regular passage migrant more so now than in Pashley's time.
Has occurred annually over the past few years in small numbers, usually no more than 10 between May and September.

White-rumped Sandpiper *(Calidris fuscicollis)*
Rare visitor. Cley October 1st and 2nd 1948, July 28th to 30th 1961, August 11th to 15th 1973, October 14th 1980 (ninth county record), July 25th 1982.
There have been four further records in the past 10 years in August or September.

Baird's Sandpiper *(Calidris bairdii)*
Rare visitor. First record for Cley, September 18th to 20th 1970; Cley, September 16th to October 10th 1971; Salthouse August 22nd 1982.

Pectoral Sandpiper *(Calidris melanotos)*
Can now be described as a scarce but regular autumn visitor and rare as a spring visitor.
Since the mid-eighties has continued to appear almost annually in autumn (between July and October), while spring visits have occurred only in 1986, 1992 and 1993.

Curlew Sandpiper *(Calidris ferruginea)*
Regular passage migrant in varying numbers to coastal marshes and mudflats. Seen quite often in full summer dress in both May and July.
From August to October numbers are made up largely of juveniles.

Purple Sandpiper *(Calidris maritima)*
Scarce but regular passage migrant and winter visitor.
Mostly seen in small numbers in September and October.

Dunlin *(Calidris alpina)*
An abundant passage migrant and winter visitor. Like the Knot, seen in large flocks. A pair bred on Salthouse Marshes in 1939.
Numbers on the Reserve reach several hundred in the autumn, while up to 4000 may overwinter around Blakeney Harbour.

Broad-billed Sandpiper *(Limicola falcinellus)*
Rare visitor. Two at Cley on August 13th 1895; Cley, June 1933 and June 1955; Salthouse, August 25th 1972 and Cley September 28th to 31st 1973, May 26th 1982, July 23rd to 27th 1982.
There have been just seven sporadic records since.

Buff-breasted Sandpiper *(Tryngites subruficollis)*
Rare visitor. Blakeney Point, September 7th 1899; Cley, May 11th to 12th 1964; Salthouse, October 3rd to 6th 1970; Cley, September 1st to 9th 1973, September 5th 1981 and May 1982.
There have been three further records in May 1984, July/August 1986 and August 1993.

Ruff *(Philomachus pugnax)*
Now a regular summer resident and passage migrant in small numbers. Present at Cley all the year and, I have suspected, breeding these past three years.
'Lekking' males are observed most years during May, but breeding has not been proved. Numbers can reach around 150 in both spring and autumn.

Jack Snipe *(Limnocryptes minimus)*
Regular winter visitor and passage migrant.
Small numbers can be observed, usually between late September and mid-April.

Snipe *(Gallinago gallinago)*
Breeding species in small numbers on fresh-water marshes and river banks, also common winter visitor and passage migrant.
A few breeding pairs. Peak winter numbers of around 300 in October and November.

Great Snipe *(Gallinago media)*
Rare passage migrant. The last one I am aware of was shot at Salthouse on September 18th 1976. I bought it for five shillings and it is now in Norwich Castle Museum.
The only more recent record is of an immature between August 25th and 27th 1987.

Long-billed Dowitcher *(Limnodromus scolopaceus)*
Rare visitor. Weybourne October 30th and Cley November 2nd to 4th 1969 (third county record).
*A bird observed at Cley and Salthouse from October 5th to November 3rd 1957 was originally thought to be a Short-billed Dowitcher (*Limnodromus griseus*). It was, however, subsequently identified from photographs as a Long-billed Dowitcher.*

Woodcock *(Scolopax rusticola)*
Regular winter visitor in varying numbers, also breeding resident.
Exceptional numbers were recorded in the winter of 1984/5 (27) and in October 1988 (18 migrants on Blakeney Point). There were also large numbers in the area over the winter of 1995/6.

Black-tailed Godwit *(Limosa limosa)*
These birds have been trying to become established as a breeding species since 1965 and have rarely been successful; they are not good parents in their methods of rearing their chicks, leading them through reed-beds and dykes at a very early age causing a high rate of mortality for young chicks.
Flocks of 30 or so are common during the summer months, though further attempts at breeding have met with limited success. Large flocks of the Icelandic race 'islandica' passed through Norfolk in spring 1994, when 780 were present on the Reserve on April 16th.

CHECKLIST

Bar-tailed Godwit *(Limosa lapponica)*
Common passage migrant.
Passing flocks of several hundred are common in both spring and autumn. A few individuals remain for the summer in some years.

Little Whimbrel *(Numenius minutus)*
A first record for England in 1985 when a juvenile was observed at Cley, Blakeney Point and Salthouse from August 24th to September 2nd.

Whimbrel *(Numenius phaeopus)*
Common passage migrant.
Normally occurs between April and October. Flocks of 20-30 can sometimes be found on the grazing marsh beyond the East Bank. Blakeney Harbour may hold flocks of 250 or so.

Curlew *(Numenius arquata)*
Common passage migrant and winter visitor.
Several hundred overwinter around Blakeney Harbour. A few non-breeding birds can usually be seen during the summer months.

Spotted Redshank *(Tringa erythropus)*
Passage migrant in moderate numbers; occasionally stays in winter.
Up to 30 birds are usually present in April/May and from July to October.

Redshank *(Tringa totanus)*
Common resident nesting in good numbers.

Marsh Sandpiper *(Tringa stagnatilis)*
Rare visitor. First county record at Cley August 14th to 18th 1979; also July 1982.
Vagrants have been recorded in May 1983, August/September 1984 and July/August 1987.

Greenshank *(Tringa nebularia)*
Regular passage migrant in moderate numbers.
Regularly occurs between April and October. Most numerous in August and September when peaks of around 50 have been recorded.

Lesser Yellowlegs *(Tringa flavipes)*
Extremely rare North American vagrant which has been recorded twice at Cley, May 28th - 29th 1992 and May 13th - 15th 1994.

CLEY MARSH AND ITS BIRDS

Solitary Sandpiper *(Tringa solitaria)*
Rare visitor. Cley September 3rd to 24th 1947.

Green Sandpiper *(Tringa ochropus)*
Regular passage migrant in small numbers; often the first wader seen on return migration.
Most likely to be seen in May, June and August. A record count of 34 was recorded on July 31st 1991.

Wood Sandpiper *(Tringa glareola)*
Regular passage migrant in small numbers.
Occasionally larger numbers occur as in July 1980 (50).

Terek Sandpiper *(Xenus cinereus)*
Rare visitor. First record for Cley July 2nd to 4th 1975, second record for Cley May 14th to 20th 1982.
The only other subsequent record was May 23rd to 29th 1983.

Common Sandpiper *(Actitis hypoleucos)*
Regular passage migrant in moderate numbers.
Peak months are July and August when up to 50 may be present.

Spotted Sandpiper *(Actitis macularia)*
Rare visitor. Perhaps the rarest bird I ever found. Cley June 7th to 8th 1957.
Recorded subsequently in May 1983 and June 1986.

Turnstone *(Arenaria interpres)*
Common passage migrant and winter visitor.
Up to 100 overwinter, mainly around Blakeney Harbour.

Wilson's Phalarope *(Phalaropus tricolor)*
Rare visitor. First Cley record May 17th 1979.
This North American phalarope was again recorded in July 1983, August 1985 and May 1987.

Red-necked Phalarope *(Phalaropus lobatus)*
Scarce passage migrant.
Has been recorded annually since the mid-eighties. Usually in August or September.

CHECKLIST

Grey Phalarope *(Phalaropus fulicarius)*
Scarce passage migrant, occasional winter visitor.
A few are seen annually, mostly from September to December when strong onshore winds are blowing.

Pomarine Skua *(Stercorarius pomarinus)*
Regular autumn visitor in small numbers.
Largest movements coincide with northerly gales. There were exceptional counts of 100 or more in October 1970 and November 1985.

Arctic Skua *(Stercorarius parasiticus)*
Common autumn passage migrant. Occasional spring visitor.
Offshore movements of 100 - 250 some years, usually in August and September during northerly gales.

Long-tailed Skua *(Stercorarius longicaudus)*
Regular autumn visitor.
A few are observed flying past offshore most years from late July to early October.

Great Skua *(Stercorarius skua)*
Regular autumn visitor in small numbers.
Counts of 100 - 200 in September and October some years, almost always coinciding with strong northerlies.

Mediterranean Gull *(Larus melanocephalus)*
Scarce, but now a regular passage migrant. Last date Cley March 30th 1970.
Now a regular year-round visitor, though normally only seen in ones and twos. Bred for the first time on Blakeney Point in 1992 and each year since.

Laughing Gull *(Larus atricilla)*
The only record of this North American vagrant is of a first-summer bird which was first seen at Salthouse on June 1st 1995. Moving west, it paused briefly on the Reserve and was seen later in Blakeney Harbour.

Little Gull *(Larus minutus)*
Regular passage migrant in varying numbers this is yet another bird that could settle to breed in the area.
Immature birds are regularly seen on the Reserve between May and July. Larger numbers may be seen passing offshore in the autumn.

CLEY MARSH AND ITS BIRDS

Sabine's Gull *(Larus sabini)*
Rare visitor. Scarce but now a regular passage migrant.
Single birds seen offshore in the autumn some years when strong northerlies are blowing.

Bonaparte's Gull *(Larus philadelphia)*
Rare visitor. Second county record on September 26th 1970.

Black-headed Gull *(Larus ridibundus)*
Very common and breeds in good numbers.
Large numbers breed on Blakeney Point, a few pairs on the Reserve.

Slender-billed Gull *(Larus genei)*
Very rare vagrant from southern Europe. An adult pair on the Reserve May 12th to 15th 1987 is the only Norfolk record.

Ring-billed Gull *(Larus delawarensis)*
This North American vagrant has been recorded once - on Pat's Pool on May 1st 1992.

Common Gull *(Larus canus)*
Abundant passage migrant.
Now present throughout the year. A few pairs nest on Blakeney Point.

Lesser Black-backed Gull *(Larus fuscus)*
Abundant passage migrant and non-breeding visitor throughout the year.
A few pairs have nested on Blakeney Point in recent years.

Herring Gull *(Larus argentatus)*
Abundant passage migrant.
Numbers have been on the increase, and a few pairs have bred regularly on Blakeney Point since 1973.

Icelandic Gull *(Larus glaucoides)*
Very scarce and irregular winter visitor.
There have been 21 records since the early seventies.

Glaucous Gull *(Larus hyperboreus)*
Scarce, but now a regular winter visitor.
Singles may occur between August and April.

Great Black-backed Gull *(Larus marinus)*
Very common.
Present throughout the year. Numbers reach around 300 in Blakeney Harbour in the winter.

Ross's Gull *(Rhodostethia rosea)*
A first Norfolk record of this Siberian vagrant at Cley between May 9th and 12th 1984.

Kittiwake *(Rissa tridactyla)*
Regular visitor in varying numbers.
Recorded throughout the year. Large numbers may be seen passing offshore in September and October, especially during northerly gales.

Gull-billed Tern *(Gelochelidon nilotica)*
Rare visitor. Pashley does not report any, but Richardson reports three. Since 1961 nine have been recorded, the last date Cley August 28th 1977.
One further record July 20th 1980.

Caspian Tern *(Sterna caspia)*
Rare visitor. Arnold's Marsh June 10th 1966, July 8th 1967 and July 13th 1968, Cley August 6th 1969 and Weybourne September 11th 1969.
There have been four subsequent records of this Baltic vagrant, the most recent on July 22nd 1990.

Lesser Crested Tern *(Sterna bengalensis)*
First English record of this very rare vagrant from N.E. Africa at Cley and Blakeney August 9th to September 17th 1983. One further record of an adult on Arnold's Marsh August 26th 1988.

Sandwich Tern *(Sterna sandvicensis)*
Common breeding summer visitor and abundant passage migrant. First bred at Salthouse (Arnold's Marsh) 1920 and bred there regularly till a saltwater flood in 1943. After one year breeding in the middle of a minefield on Cley Beach they moved to Blakeney Point, and except for an odd pair they have not returned to their original breeding area.
The breeding colony on Blakeney Point is now well established. Numbers fluctuate, but since the mid-seventies in excess of 3000 pairs have bred there. At Cley up to 500 may be seen on Arnold's Marsh, particularly in spring and autumn.

CLEY MARSH AND ITS BIRDS

Roseate Tern *(Sterna dougallii)*
Rare passage migrant, has been known to breed locally, but not since 1948.
Single birds now recorded most years between May and September. One pair stayed all summer in 1993 and two pairs in 1994 but did not breed.

Common Tern *(Sterna hirundo)*
Common summer visitor, breeds in large numbers on the National Trust Reserve at Blakeney Point
This colony has been established since at least the early 19th Century. Numbers have declined over the past 50 years from about 2000 pairs to a stable 200 - 300 pairs in recent years. A few pairs nest on the Reserve.

Arctic Tern *(Sterna paradisaea)*
Scarce but regular summer visitor known to interbreed with Common Tern.
A few pairs breed on Blakeney Point. At Cley they are mainly seen passing offshore in spring and autumn.

Sooty Tern *(Sterna fuscata)*
Rare visitor; one at Blakeney on September 11th 1935 and another on June 14th 1966.

Little Tern *(Sterna albifrons)*
Breeding summer visitor in small numbers.
In excess of 100 pairs breed on Blakeney Point some years.

Whiskered Tern *(Chlidonias hybridus)*
Rare visitor. One seen at Cley May 24th 1947.
Two adults were observed on Pat's Pool on May 22nd 1994.

Black Tern *(Chlidonias niger)*
Regular passage migrant. This is a bird that I think will again breed if suitable habitat can be maintained.
Most records fall in May and September. Largest numbers occur with easterly winds. An exceptional 1000+ were observed at Cley on May 2nd 1990. Numbers on autumn passage are much smaller.

White-winged Black Tern *(Chlidonias leucopterus)*
Rare visitor. Pashley had never had one in the flesh and Richardson reports twelve. Since 1961, twelve have been reported; one was at Cley June 2nd to 9th 1977, and again in 1982.
There were three subsequent records in August 1986, July 1989 and November 1994.

Guillemot *(Uria aalge)*
Regular passage migrant and winter visitor in moderate numbers.
Largest numbers normally from September to November. 'Wrecks' occur occasionally (most notably in February 1983), the result of bad weather or pollution. There was a remarkable movement around the Norfolk coast on February 20th 1994 when 2000 or so Guillemots and Razorbills were seen flying east at Cley.

Razorbill *(Alca torda)*
Regular passage migrant.
Usually less numerous than Guillemot.

Black Guillemot *(Cepphus grylle)*
Scarce but regular winter visitor.
Odd birds are recorded most years between September and May.

Little Auk *(Alle alle)*
Scarce visitor, mostly with offshore gales.
A few are normally seen offshore from September to April, though northerly winds in October/November can result in passages of up to 200. A massive and unprecedented movement began on October 29th 1995 when about 300 passed offshore. Numbers increased over the next few days and peaked at about 1200+ on November 2nd (see Diary entry).

Puffin *(Fratercula arctica)*
Winter visitor in small numbers.
A few offshore from September to April. 35 corpses were recorded between Blakeney Point and Cley Coastguards in the 'wreck' of February 1983. An exceptional 22 were seen at Cley on September 14th 1994.

Pallas's Sandgrouse *(Syrrhaptes paradoxus)*
Can be described as a wanderer. The first eruption occurred on May 30th 1863 at Morston, with approximately thirty, most of which were taken. There were a maximum of 100 at Morston, Blakeney, Cley and Langham between May 1888 and February 1889 and another flock in May 1908. No breeding records. Had these birds been protected as now they could easily have bred.

Stock Dove *(Columba oenas)*
Common passage migrant, winter visitor and breeding species.

CLEY MARSH AND ITS BIRDS

Wood Pigeon *(Columba palumbus)*
A very common and destructive pest; despite the saying, it does not migrate. I have witnessed them coming in from the sea in thousands in early morning. (See Diary entries.)

Collared Dove *(Streptopelia decaocto)*
Now a very common breeding species. Very rare before the early fifties.

Turtle Dove *(Streptopelia turtur)*
Common passage migrant and breeding visitor.
Small flocks are often seen flying west over the Reserve in May and June.

Ring-necked Parakeet *(Psittacula krameri)*
Eleven records of this introduced species.

Great Spotted Cuckoo *(Clamator glandarius)*
Very rare south European vagrant. Two records in the area. Seen between Cley and Salthouse in October 1977, and at Blakeney Point in July 1992.

Cuckoo *(Cuculus canorus)*
Common. Visits the Reserve regularly to deposit their eggs in reed warblers' nests.

Barn Owl *(Tyto alba)*
Scarce. Breeding resident.
About five pairs breed in the area. There have been just four records of the dark-breasted continental race guttata.

Scops Owl *(Otus scops)*
Rare visitor. One near Holt on November 18th 1892 and one at Blakeney Point on October 6th 1922. One thought to be heard at Cley in September 1977.

Snowy Owl *(Nyctea scandiaca)*
One on Blakeney Point March 23rd 1991 - the only record for the area.

Little Owl *(Athene noctua)*
A breeding resident in much smaller numbers than twenty-five years ago and decreasing all the time.
Has not bred in the area since the early 1960's. Single birds are occasionally seen around the village.

Tawny Owl *(Strix aluco)*
Most woods in the area hold their pair of Tawny Owls.

Long-eared Owl *(Asio otus)*
A breeding resident and a passage migrant but not in large numbers.

Short-eared Owl *(Asio flammeus)*
A scarce breeding resident and large numbers come in during late autumn at the same time as Woodcock, and is locally called the Woodcock Owl.

Nightjar *(Caprimulgus europaeus)*
Common breeding bird in local heathland.
About half a dozen pairs breed in the area.

Swift *(Apus apus)*
Abundant summer visitor.

Pacific Swift *(Apus pacificus)*
First British record at Cley May 30th 1993. Remained over the Reserve most of the day with a large migrant flock of common swifts.

Alpine Swift *(Apus melba)*
Rare visitor. Six records Cley and Blakeney.
Now 17 records in total, up to April 1994.

Kingfisher *(Alcedo atthis)*
Breeding resident in small numbers. Numbers often reduced in very hard weather.

Bee-eater *(Merops apiaster)*
Rare visitor. Two at Blakeney April 26th 1960 and one at Cley the same day.
Four subsequent records in the Cley/Blakeney area.

Hoopoe *(Upupa epops)*
Scarce but regular passage migrant, often seen on local lawns.
A total of twelve records since the early 1970's.

Wryneck *(Jynx torquilla)*
Scarce, but regular passage migrant. Bred at Blakeney in 1925.
A few occur most years, usually in August and September, occasionally in spring.

Green Woodpecker *(Picus viridis)*
Breeding resident in small numbers. Frequent visitor to open marshes in winter.

Great Spotted Woodpecker *(Dendrocopos major)*
Breeding resident in small numbers in local deciduous woods.

Lesser Spotted Woodpecker *(Dendrocopos minor)*
Scarce breeding resident.
Nesting in local woodlands, they are sometimes seen on the Reserve.

Short-toed Lark *(Calandrella brachydactyla)*
One at Cley, October 14th 1959, which was filmed by R. Bagnall-Oakeley, one at Salthouse, September 8th 1977, three at Cley, September 25th to October 16th 1977; one at Cley on October 20th 1977, and one at Weybourne October 14th and 15th 1978.
Five subsequent records for the area.

Woodlark *(Lullula arborea)*
Much rarer in the area than twenty-five years ago. I saw the last nest on the Hangs in 1956.
Now seen fairly regularly on spring or, more usually, autumn passage.

Skylark *(Alauda arvensis)*
Very common.

Shorelark *(Eremophila alpestris)*
Usually arrive in late September and leave during the following April. Regular migrants.
Numbers have declined drastically in recent years.

Sand Martin *(Riparia riparia)*
Abundant summer visitor.

Swallow *(Hirundo rustica)*
Common summer visitors.
Very large numbers roost in the reed-beds in the autumn.

Red-rumped Swallow *(Hirundo daurica)*
One seen March 6th to 22nd 1952; again on June 11th 1977.
Spring records (April/May) in 1980, 1987 and 1990. Also November 12th - 14th 1994.

House Martin *(Delichon urbica)*
Abundant summer visitor.

Richard's Pipit *(Anthus novaeseelandiae)*
Scarce. Autumn visitor usually in October.

Tawny Pipit *(Anthus campestris)*
Rare visitor. No more than ten records.
Has occurred fairly regularly in recent years, mainly on Blakeney Point. Recorded in the Eye Field in June 1991 and May 1994.

Olive-backed Pipit *(Anthus hodgsoni)*
Siberian vagrant. Two records on Blakeney Point October 1987 and 1990.

Tree Pipit *(Anthus trivialis)*
Summer visitor. Breeds in small numbers on heathland and plantation in young conifers.

Meadow Pipit *(Anthus pratensis)*
Common breeding bird and resident.

Red-throated Pipit *(Anthus cervinus)*
Rare north European vagrant. Has occurred annually in the area since 1987. Cley records in May 1982, 1989 and 1992. Also November 1994.

Rock Pipit *(Anthus petrosus)*
Regular autumn visitor.
Usually present from September to April. The Scandinavian race littoralis *occurs regularly in early spring.*

Water Pipit *(Anthus spinoletta)*
First taken locally by M. Catlin 1905. A bird I have often thought is overlooked. I have seen odd birds at Blakeney.
As many as 30 have overwintered on the Reserve in recent years, a few staying on until March or April.

Yellow Wagtail *(Motacilla flava flavissima)*
Breeds in fair numbers on Cley and Salthouse Reserves, arriving in mid-April.
Flocks of up to 300 may be seen in August/September. Much smaller numbers on spring passage, though occasional falls of 300-400 birds have occurred as in April 1986 and 1987.

There have been records of birds showing characteristics of the following geographic races of this exceptionally variable species:

Blue-headed Wagtail *(Motacilla flava flava)*
Seen most years in spring and occasionally in autumn. First record September 1st 1980.
A handful of birds are usually seen in May or early June and sometimes in September.

Grey-headed Wagtail *(Motacilla flava thunbergi)*
Rare passage migrant. No more than ten records.
Small numbers are now recorded most years usually in May and June. Ten were seen on the Eye Field May 14th 1992.

Black-headed Wagtail *(Motacilla flava feldegg)*
Rare visitor. One seen at Cley on June 17th to 19th 1910, April 13th 1939 and May 17th 1973.
Also recorded July 23rd to August 11th 1983.

Birds showing characteristics of the south European race cinereocapilla *(**Ashy-headed Wagtail**) and the central Asian race* beema *(**Sykes' Wagtail**) are seen from time to time, though very rarely. My father recorded the former in April or May in 1955, 1964 and 1976. There have been five records of the latter. Interbreeding of the races of* flava *wagtails often makes identification somewhat uncertain.*

Citrine Wagtail *(Motacilla citreola)*
One local record September 26th - 29th 1986 at Blakeney.

Grey Wagtail *(Motacilla cinerea)*
More common than a few years ago.
No more than a few are seen each year on spring or autumn passage.

Pied Wagtail *(Motacilla alba yarrellii)*
Fairly common breeding bird and resident.
The continental race 'alba' *(White Wagtail) is an annual passage migrant in spring.*

CHECKLIST

Waxwing *(Bombycilla garrulus)*
Irregular winter visitor, sometimes in fair numbers. Recent Waxwing years, 1965, 1966, 1970, 1974.
No further records until 1984, but then recorded annually in the area usually in October or November until 1991, and again in 1994. 1988 was an exceptional year when 40+ were seen at Cley and Wiveton at the end of October; and an unusually late influx occurred in January 1996. From around the 5th to the end of the month parties of up to 46 were seen around Cley, Wiveton and Glandford.

Dipper *(Cinclus cinclus)*
Rare visitor. Most of those found locally are the black-bellied form.
The only recent Cley record is April 7th 1984.

Wren *(Troglodytes troglodytes)*
Common. Numbers often reduced in hard winters.

Dunnock *(Prunella modularis)*
Common.
Breeding resident and passage migrant.

Robin *(Erithacus rubecula)*
Abundant breeding resident.
Large falls of the continental race rubecula *occur from time to time in late autumn as on October 11th 1951 (see Diary). More recently a fall of about 200 on Blakeney Point in October 1990.*

Thrush Nightingale *(Luscinia luscinia)*
Very rare vagrant. Three local records: May 1988 (Blakeney Point), May 1989 (Cley) and September 1992 (Salthouse).

Nightingale *(Luscinia megarhynchos)*
Spring migrant; breeds in thick woods and heathland in small numbers.
Usually present from April to August. Salthouse Heath is a favourite location.

Bluethroat (Red-spotted) *(Luscinia svecica svecica)*
Scarce but regular passage migrant.
Occurs most years in small numbers along the beach, usually in spring. There were exceptional falls of 20+ in 1985 and 1987.

Bluethroat (White-spotted) *(Luscinia svecica cyanecula)*
Rare visitor.
Only four Norfolk records.

Black Redstart *(Phoenicurus ochruros)*
Often one of the earliest spring arrivals and now breeds in Norfolk. Major Daukes and myself found them breeding at Weybourne in 1955.
Continues to breed in the county in small numbers. A pair bred at Salthouse in 1986.

Redstart *(Phoenicurus phoenicurus)*
Arrives sometimes in great numbers in autumn.
Much smaller numbers on spring passage.

Whinchat *(Saxicola rubetra)*
Common passage migrant. I do not know of any record of it breeding locally.
Most numerous on autumn passage.

Stonechat *(Saxicola torquata)*
Regular passage migrant and quite often a winter resident on the reserve. Bred locally before the Second World War; last breeding record was at Morston in 1961.
There have been further records of breeding in the Salthouse and Weybourne area. Often seen on the Reserve near reed-cutters in the winter.

Siberian Stonechat *(Saxicola torquata maura/stejnegei)*
Very rare visitor. One seen at Cley on May 22nd 1972.
Since 1986 almost annual September/October records in the area.

Wheatear *(Oenanthe oenanthe)*
Common spring migrant and breeds locally.
Often seen locally in quite large numbers (up to 100) in both spring and autumn. Birds of the Greenland race leucorrhoa *are sometimes identified.*

Pied Wheatear *(Oenanthe pleschanka)*
A single record at Blakeney Point October 16th 1988.

Black-eared Wheatear *(Oenanthe hispanica)*
First county record at Salthouse August 30th to September 14th 1965; again at Cley on May 13th 1975.
Also October 17th 1988 at Salthouse.

CHECKLIST

Desert Wheatear *(Oenanthe deserti)*
The first of these species was taken by M. Catling on October 31st 1907; it was the first county record. The second county record was found at Cley beach on October 14th 1978.
Recorded again at Cley on November 6th 1994.

Rock Thrush *(Monticola saxatilis)*
Very rare visitor. First county record May 9th 1969 Salthouse heath.

Ring Ouzel *(Turdus torquatus)*
Regular bird in spring and autumn.
A few are seen each year, mostly during April/May and in September/October.

Blackbird *(Turdus merula)*
Very common breeding resident; also a great many on autumn passage.

Fieldfare *(Turdus pilaris)*
Common winter visitor, heard singing on the wing during migration.
Large numbers are often seen flying in from the sea in autumn.

Song-thrush *(Turdus philomelos)*
Abundant breeding resident in every village garden.
Numbers have declined markedly over recent years. Birds of the continental race 'Philomelos' sometimes migrate to the coast in quite large numbers.

Redwing *(Turdus iliacus)*
Abundant winter visitor.
Large migrant flocks may be seen passing through in both spring and autumn.

Mistle Thrush *(Turdus viscivorus)*
Breeding resident and possibly autumn bird of passage.
Much less common than the song thrush.

Cetti's Warbler *(Cettia cetti)*
A rare vagrant beyond the established Broadland breeding colony. Recorded at Cley on November 15th 1981 and from November 12th to December 4th 1993.

Fan-tailed Warbler *(Cisticola juncidis)*
Cley August 24th 1976. First British record of this diminutive warbler that has spread across Europe since 1970.

Pallas's Grasshopper Warbler *(Locustella certhiola)*
Cley, May 13th 1976. First County record. Breeds in Western Siberia and Central Asia and only the fourth British record.

Grasshopper Warbler *(Locustella naevia)*
Heard and seen most years. Breeds in small numbers.

Savi's Warbler *(Locuetella luscinioides)*
Very rare summer vagrant. In recent years, has occurred in May 1987, 1990 and 1992.

Aquatic Warbler *(Acrocephalus paludicola)*
Scarce autumn migrant.
Only two records in recent years: August 13th 1985 and October 11th 1994.

Sedge Warbler *(Acrocephalus schoenobaenus)*
Like Reed Warbler breeds in fair numbers on the Reserve.

Marsh Warbler *(Acrocephalus palustris)*
Very rare vagrant. Two June records at Cley in 1985 and 1992.

Reed Warbler *(Acrocephalus scirpaceus)*
Common breeding bird on the Reserve.

Great Reed Warbler *(Acrocephalus arundinaceus)*
Very rare vagrant. Recorded at Cley June 8th to 24th 1988, and from May 11th to June 27th 1994.

Icterine Warbler *(Hippolais icterina)*
Scarce passage migrant.
Occurs most years in very small numbers. Mostly recorded on Blakeney Point.

Melodious Warbler *(Hippolais polyglotta)*
Very rare visitor. Seen at Cley June 7th and September 5th 1957.

Dartford Warbler *(Sylvia undata)*
One recorded on Blakeney Point May 17th - 19th 1986.

Subalpine Warbler *(Sylvia cantillans)*
Rare visitor. Seen at Cley June 11th 1951, Blakeney Point September 29th 1955 and May 22nd to 23rd, and at Lower Bodham on April 10th 1974. Fourth county record.
There have been no more than half a dozen subsequent local records of this Mediterranean vagrant.

Barred Warbler *(Sylvia nisoria)*
Not so scarce in recent years as formerly; now seen fairly regularly.
Two or three birds are seen most years in the autumn (August to October).

Desert Warbler *(Sylvia nana)*
First British spring record on Blakeney Point May 27th to June 1st 1993.

Lesser Whitethroat *(Sylvia curruca)*
Not so common as Whitethroat, but fairly plentiful in some areas.
Breeds locally each year in fair numbers.

Siberian Lesser Whitethroat *(Sylvia curruca blythi)*
Rare autumn visitor. Seen at Blakeney Point August 26th 1954, September 16th 1956, September 17th 1959 and September 9th 1961.

Whitethroat *(Sylvia communis)*
Nests in fair numbers.

Garden Warbler *(Sylvia borin)*
Common in Autumn and breeds in small numbers.

Blackcap *(Sylvia atricapilla)*
Nests in fair numbers.
Good numbers on autumn passage some years. A few birds overwinter.

Greenish Warbler *(Phylloscopus trochiloides)*
Rare visitor. Seen at Blakeney Point September 6th 1951 and August 12th 1977.
Since recorded in August/September in 1987, 1990, 1991 and 1992, all on Blakeney Point. Vagrant from north-east Europe.

Arctic Warbler *(Phylloscopus borealis)*
Rare visitor. Seen at Blakeney Point September 4th 1922, September 21st 1951, August 24th to 31st 1968, September 20th 1977; and at Weybourne on September 22nd 1977.
One further record of this north European vagrant at the Watch House, Blakeney Point on September 1st and 2nd 1993.

Pallas's Warbler *(Phylloscopus proregulus)*
The first record for the British Isles was taken (shot) by Ted Ramm on October 31st 1896, and the only other that I am aware of was recorded at Cley on October 31st 1976.
Eight further records between 1984 and 1994, all in October or November.

Yellow-browed Warbler *(Phylloscopus inornatus)*
The first taken at Cley on October 1st 1894 was the fourth record for the British Isles. Latest dates are at Cley, September 21st to 23rd 1962 and October 1st 1979; and at Blakeney Point, September 24th to 27th 1973 and September 20th 1977.
Has occurred fairly regularly in September or October since the early eighties.

Radde's Warbler *(Phylloscopus schwarzi)*
Rare visitor. Seen at Blakeney Point October 3rd to 5th 1961.
Central Asian vagrant. Occurred in October 1988 on Blakeney Point and October 1991 at Kelling Quag.

Dusky Warbler *(Phylloscopus fuscatus)*
Blakeney Point October 18th 1975, fifth county record.
Five further October/November records in the area of this central Asian vagrant.

Bonelli's Warbler *(Phylloscopus bonelli)*
Very rare vagrant from central and southern Europe. One recorded on Blakeney Point May 14th 1988.

Wood Warbler *(Phylloscopus sibilatrix)*
Becoming a scarce breeding summer visitor.
A few pairs breed in the area, though not every year. The odd migrant is seen from time to time.

Chiffchaff *(Phylloscopus collybita)*
Often the first of the spring visitors. Quite common.

Willow Warbler *(Phylloscopus trochilus)*
Common breeding bird. The northern race *'acredula'*, a regular passage migrant in small numbers.

Goldcrest *(Regulus regulus)*
Breeding resident.
Most numerous on autumn passage between September and November, with occasional large 'falls'.

Firecrest *(Regulus ignicapillus)*
Scarce breeding resident.
Nowadays occurs only as a passage migrant in small numbers.

Spotted Flycatcher *(Muscicapa striata)*
Common breeding species.
Has declined as a breeding species but occurs in good numbers on autumn passage (August/September).

Red-breasted Flycatcher *(Ficedula parva)*
Rather scarce autumn passage migrant.
A few are seen most years in September or October.

Collared Flycatcher *(Ficedula albicollis)*
An extremely rare vagrant from central and south-eastern Europe. First local record on May 5th 1995 when one was seen along the East Bank and later briefly in a garden near the Visitor Centre. The second record for the county.

Pied Flycatcher *(Ficedula hypoleuca)*
More common whilst on passage in the autumn than spring.
East winds sometimes result in autumn falls of 50 or more.

Bearded Tit *(Panurus biarmicus)*
Now a breeding resident. Major Daukes and I found them breeding at Cley again after forty years in 1948.
Has bred on the Reserve annually since 1956. Numbers peaked in the 1980's at around 50 pairs. Fewer nowadays - probably about ten pairs.

Long-tailed Tit *(Aegithalos caudatus)*
Breeding resident and possibly passage migrant. I once saw a party with white heads in the reeds on Cley Reserve, thought to be of the northern race, in October 1961.

CLEY MARSH AND ITS BIRDS

Marsh Tit *(Parus palustris)*
Breeding resident in small numbers.

Willow Tit *(Parus montanus)*
Breeding resident in small numbers.
Numbers have declined and is now rare in the area.

Coal Tit *(Parus ater)*
Breeding resident in smaller numbers.

Blue Tit *(Parus caeruleus)*
Abundant.

Great Tit *(Parus major)*
Common breeding bird and resident.
The continental race 'major' *is sometimes observed on autumn passage.*

Nuthatch *(Sitta europaea)*
As with Tree Creeper, more common in thickly wooded areas inland.

Tree Creeper *(Certhia familiaris)*
Quite common a few miles inland.

Penduline Tit *(Remiz pendulinus)*
Extremely rare vagrant. One Cley record October 13th 1990.

Golden Oriole *(Oriolus oriolus)*
Rare visitor. I have seen only two in the area but they now breed in Eastern Counties.
About ten local records since the early eighties, almost all in late May or early June.

Red-backed Shrike *(Lanius collurio)*
Breeding summer visitor in declining numbers; also a scarce passage migrant.
No longer breeds locally, but a few birds are seen in the area most years on both spring and autumn passage.

Lesser Grey Shrike *(Lanius minor)*
Rare visitor. One at Salthouse May 15th to 16th 1960 and one at Cley September 5th to 6th 1976.

CHECKLIST

Great Grey Shrike *(Lanius excubitor)*
Scarce but regular winter visitor to local heathland.

Woodchat Shrike *(Lanius senator)*
Rare spring visitor. Under ten records, the last record at Cley 1977.
Only two further local records: May 1992 (Blakeney Point) and June/July 1993 (Kelling).

Jay *(Garrulus glandarius)*
Common in wooded areas but they are very secretive and not seen often. Gamekeepers undoubtedly keep these handsome thieves in check.
Occasional invasions of continental birds as in October 1983 when 134 were counted at Walsey Hills and 63 at Cley, all flying west. Another influx occurred in 1993 when 70 were seen heading west at Cley on September 25th.

Magpie *(Pica pica)*
Common in areas that are not keepered, as they are an enemy of game chicks and eggs, and are not difficult for gamekeepers to destroy.

Nutcracker *(Nucifraga caryocatactes)*
Pashley reports three in his records. Richardson does not report any. An invasion occurred in 1968 (see Diary) when 104 were reported in Norfolk from 58 areas. Only two were reported at Cley September 29th 1968.

Jackdaw *(Corvus monedula)*
A common breeding bird and, like the Rook, many arrive in the autumn.
Breeds in the village.

Rook *(Corvus frugilegus)*
There are many rookeries in this part of the coast and large numbers pass along to the west on passage in the autumn.

Carrion Crow *(Corvus corone)*
Breeds in the area and quite common.

Hooded Crow *(Corvus corone cornix)*
Not such a common winter visitor as twenty years ago but a regular bird of passage in the autumn.
Single birds are seen most years.

Raven *(Corvus corax)*
I have never personally seen or heard of one in the area. Pashley reports one within four miles of Cley with no date and Richardson reports seven between 1933 and 1953. One was seen at Weybourne on October 5th 1972.
No records since.

Starling *(Sturnus vulgaris)*
Very common. Flocks of many thousands invade the area during the autumn; also a common breeding bird.
These enormous autumn flocks roost in the reed-beds and can cause considerable damage to the reed.

Rose-coloured Starling *(Sturnus roseus)*
Rare visitor. Pashley reports one and Richardson two. I have only seen one since the last publication of Checklist, May 19th to May 27th 1979, at first on the Hangs and later in a village garden. Later seen by many observers.
A juvenile was seen at the Watch House on August 22nd 1983.

House Sparrow *(Passer domesticus)*
Very common.

Tree Sparrow *(Passer montanus)*
Breeds in the area. Flocks pass through in autumn.
Now breeds in very small numbers. Seems to have decreased.

Rock Sparrow *(Petronia petronia)*
Very rare. First county record June 14th 1981.

Chaffinch *(Fringilla coelebs)*
Common.
Very large flocks are sometimes seen on autumn passage.

Brambling *(Fringilla montifringilla)*
Winter visitor sometimes in large numbers.
Flocks of up to 300 or so are seen some years.

Serin *(Serinus serinus)*
Very rare vagrant. Recorded just twice - in May 1992 and June 1993.

Greenfinch *(Carduelis chloris)*
Common breeding bird.

CHECKLIST

Goldfinch *(Carduelis carduelis)*
One of the most beautiful birds; breeds in most local orchards.

Siskin *(Carduelis spinus)*
Autumn visitor, not common by any means.
Occasional, exceptionally large movements as on October 15th 1993 when about 250 were observed flying west over the village.

Linnet *(Carduelis cannabina)*
Very plentiful. Breeds in numbers on all heathlands.
Flocks of several thousand are regularly seen moving along the beach in both spring and autumn.

Twite *(Carduelis flavirostris)*
A common bird in some years along the shore.
Numbers have declined markedly in recent years.

Redpoll *(Carduelis flammea)*
Not common. Nest found at Kelling in 1916 by J. Forstick, and one at Salthouse in an elder bush by Bernard Bishop in 1973. A few arrive in autumn.
Has become very rare in recent years.

Mealy Redpoll *(Carduelis flammea flammea)*
Irregular migrant in autumn.
Exceptional numbers occur some years. A flock of about 40 was present in the fields at Cley, March 3rd - 6th 1986.

Arctic Redpoll *(Carduelis hornemanni)*
Rare visitor. One reported at Morston, November 3rd 1945; one at Cley, January 5th 1973.
Two subsequent October records, in 1975 and 1990, and a sequence of sightings between mid-November and mid-December 1995 when at least four different individuals were seen between Blakeney Point and the Cley Bank.

Two-barred Crossbill *(Loxia leucoptera)*
One reported at Blakeney Point, September 15th 1969.

Crossbill *(Loxia curvirostra)*
More common both as a breeding species and winter visitor.
Nowadays mainly seen on passage in irruption years.

Parrott Crossbill *(Loxia pytyopsittacus)*
One was taken at Langham in 1907.
A male and four juveniles were recorded at Cley July 17th - 18th 1985.

Scarlet Rosefinch *(Carpodacus erythrinus)*
One at Blakeney Point, August 19th to 20th 1973; and one at Cley May 26th 1974. Second and third county record.
Five further local records 1992 - 94, all in late May or early June.

Bullfinch *(Pyrrhula pyrrhula)*
Much more common than a few years ago.
Though still present in only small numbers.

Hawfinch *(Coccothraustes coccothraustes)*
A scarce breeding bird but seldom seen.

Lapland Bunting *(Calcarius lapponicus)*
Regular bird in autumn.
Normally recorded in small numbers between September and April, often in the Eye Field.

Snow Bunting *(Plectrophenax nivalis)*
Regular winter visitor. Feeds on the seed of the sea poppy, often in large flocks on the landward side of the beach.
Usually to be seen from October to April. Flocks of 150 or so occur regularly along the beach between Salthouse and Blakeney Point.

Yellowhammer *(Emberiza citrinella)*
Common in most hedgerows.

Cirl Bunting *(Emberiza cirlus)*
Pashley reports six or seven, Richardson one on October 5th 1954.

Ortolan Bunting *(Emberiza hortulana)*
Scarce but regular autumn visitor; irregular in spring.
Recorded most years, mainly in August or September.

Rustic Bunting *(Emberiza rustica)*
Rare visitor. One seen at Blakeney Point, September 10th to 13th 1958; another at Blakeney Point, October 18th to 22nd 1975; and one at Cley on October 22nd 1975.
Three more local records (all in May) in 1985, 1987 and 1994.

Little Bunting *(Emberiza pusilla)*
Rare visitor. First record for county, October 19th 1908; one at Cley October 5th to 10th 1945; one at Stiffkey, October 5th 1954; one at Cley, September 27th 1976; and one at Stiffkey, September 22nd to 26th 1977.
Recorded again in the area in November 1983, and in September and November 1993.

Yellow-breasted Bunting *(Emberiza aureola)*
One was taken on September 21st 1905 and another on September 4th 1913 (both by E.C. Arnold).

Reed Bunting *(Emberiza schoeniclus)*
Common breeding bird.
Many pairs breed on the Reserve. Present throughout the year.

Black-headed Bunting *(Emberiza melanocephala)*
April 3rd 1979 and May 3rd 1979 only.

Corn Bunting *(Miliaria calandra)*
Not by any means as common as a few years ago. A few breed.
Has now more or less disappeared from the area.

Appendix

The History of Cley Marshes

In the sixteenth century, Cley Marsh consisted only of saltings, covered by the sea at high tide, with a wide navigable channel connecting Salthouse village with Cley haven and Blakeney estuary. A causeway crossed this area at the side of the present 'long drift', giving access to the 'Eye' and to the beach at low tide. The 'Eye' has been farmed as arable or pasture land since time immemorial. A description of it in a Deed of 1651 reads as follows:

> All that piece of high marsh ground in Cley aforesaid called or known by the name or names of ffoulness or East Eye conteyning by estimacon three score and ten acres with one lodge or house thereupon built.

Today, its area has been reduced by the encroaching sea to less than 30 acres. The building mentioned was thought at one time to have been a Chapel like that served by the Carmelite Friars on Blakeney Eye, but this belief is not substantiated and it is more likely to have been a farm steading.

The shingle beach at that date lay several hundred yards north of its present position. The beach has been encroaching at an estimated rate of 3 feet per year, driven inwards by flood tides, storms and scouring currents, and many acres of the original marshes, inccluding most of the old Salthouse channel bed, now lie under the open sea north of the present beach.

HISTORY OF CLEY MARSHES

The first embankment was built in 1637 by Jan Van Hasedunk, a pupil of Sir Cornelius Vermuyden, the famous Dutch engineer, who drained the Middle Level of the Fens. It was built to protect the village of Salthouse from floods rather than to reclaim land for agricultural purposes. In 1649, Simon Britiff, Lord of the Manor of Cley, erected a bank from his 'capital messuage' (now Cley Old Hall) northwards abreast the Cley channel to the west corner of the 'Eye', then from the east corner of the 'Eye' along the south edge of the Salthouse channel to a piece of raised ground and thence returning straight southwards to meet the upland. This embankment did not interfere with the navigable Salthouse or Cley channels and there is no evidence that Britiff suffered the opposition that was aroused by other local reclamation schemes. He was merely enclosing his own property to increase the value of his grazing, wildfowling and reed harvest.

The area inside these banks has altered little in character during the last 300 years. The twisting creeks of the early salt marshes can still be distinguished. The original banks have been broken and built up again after successive 'rages of the sea' which have flooded the marsh with salt water three or four times in every hundred years. Minor drainage dykes and sluices have been added for the control of water levels. But, generally speaking, the property has remained unchanged as pasture for sheep and cattle, reed beds which still provide a valuable harvest and the 'Eye' under cultivation for arable crops. Since it's embankment, Cley Marsh has been a private property with agricultural and sporting rights reserved by landowner or by farmer.

By 1850, the navigable channel to Salthouse was entirely blocked by the encroaching shingle beach and, in 1855, the 'North Drain' or 'New Cut' was dug and its existing sluices constructed to carry away salt flood water which frequently inundated Salthouse marshes. An agreement was made with the parishioners of the village that the sluice gates in the 'East Bank' should not be opened in the event of a major flood until the (more valuable) Cley Marsh had been drained of salt water.

About the same time, the present road to Cley beach was constructed. This roadway was given to Cley parish by the Cozens-Hardy family, then Lords of the Manor, in exchange for an agreement that the right of way crossing the marsh by the 'Long Drift' be closed.

In 1897, the sea broke down the north bank once again and it was repaired by the owner at considerable cost and faced with concrete. Remnants of this concrete wall can still be seen on the beach at the north end of the East Bank.

The north wall was finally broken by a bad storm in 1921 and it has not been rebuilt since that date. During World War II, gun positions were built behind the crest of the beach and mines were laid in the shingle. At the end of the war, and again after the floods in 1953 and 1976-1978, some work was done by Coastal Defence Authorities in an attempt to stabilise the beach by pile-driving and by raising the height of the shingle with bull-dozers.

It was estimated that the whole length of the beach from Kelling to Blakeney was driven inwards more than fifty yards during the great storm of 1953. A gap appeared immediately east of the 'Eye' where the flood water, covering both Cley and Salthouse marshes to a depth of over 15 feet, flowed out 'like a salmon river in spate' when the tide receded. The gun emplacements of 1940 are now smashed to pieces and their remains, together with the steel piling, are left about the high water mark on the north side of the beach.

The beach has not moved much in the last ten years but it is unstable and porous so that the small area of marsh between the shingle and the North Drain is brackish.

The main portion of the marsh is supplied with fresh water by springs from the chalk strata which come to the surface in various places along the south boundary ditch. This fills the ditches which intersect the grazing marshes and the reed beds with beautiful clear water of which there seems to be an inexhaustible supply. The surplus fresh water flows into the North Drain and thence to the sea.

In 1926, Cley Marshes were put up for sale by the executors of the late Mr Arthur Cozens-Hardy of Cley Hall.

Dr Sidney Long was very anxious that this property, so rich in bird life, should be acquired by the Norfolk Naturalists Trust of which he was founder with Mr Russell Colman as the first chairman. The Trust Council was in full agreement but had no funds available for the purchase. However, Captain Geoffrey Colman, Sir Henry Birkin, Mr

Colin McLean and some other generous sportsmen and bird lovers put up a sum sufficient to purchase the marsh and gave it to the Trust 'in the hope that, if carefully looked after during the breeding season, certain of our species might be induced to return to nest'.

Arnold's Marsh, now reduced by sea encroachment to about sixteen acres of mud, flooded by brackish water at high tides, is the last remaining piece of the old Salthouse Broads. It is ideal feeding ground for shore birds and waders which can be watched easily, without disturbance, from the northern end of the East Bank.

This area was purchased in 1932 by the late Mr E. C. Arnold, a well-known ornithologist and collector, and bequeathed in his Will to the National Trust when he died in 1949. By an agreement made in 1962, the lease of Arnold's Marsh was made over to the Norfolk Naturalists Trust and it is now managed as a part of Cley Sanctuary.

In 1964, these marshes were designated a Bird Sanctuary under the 1954 Bird Protection Act. The shooting lease ended and the present system of management was introduced.

It remains the primary intention of the Trust to preserve the character of Cley Marsh as it has existed for 300 years and to keep it as a bird sanctuary with particular attraction for rare species.

Reprinted by kind permission of Norfolk Wildlife Trust.

NOTES

NOTES

NOTES